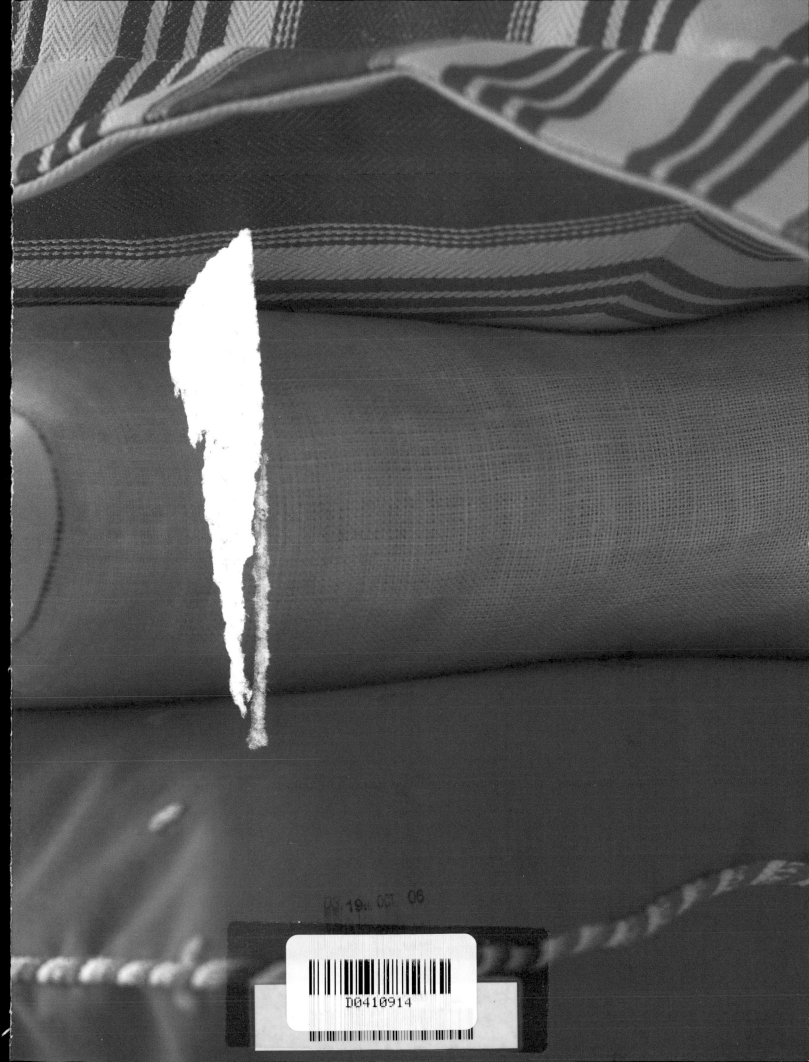

Katrin Cargill's
simple cushions

creative ideas & 20 step-by-step projects

Katrin Cargill's
simple cushions

creative ideas & 20 step-by-step projects

Katrin Cargill
photography by **James Merrell**

RYLAND
PETERS
& SMALL
LONDON NEW YORK

For this edition:

Designers Saskia Janssen and Sarah Fraser

Editor Miriam Hyslop

Production Sheila Smith

Art Director Gabriella Le Grazie

Publishing Director Alison Starling

Illustrator Jacqueline Pestell

First published in Great Britain in 1996
and reissued with amendments in 2005 by
Ryland Peters & Small
20–21 Jockey's Fields
London WC1R 4BW
www.rylandpeters.com

Text copyright © 1996, 2005 Katrin Cargill
Design and photographs copyright
© Ryland Peters & Small 1996, 2005

Printed in China.

The author's moral rights have been asserted. All rights
reserved. No part of this publication may be reproduced,
stored in a retrieval system or transmitted in any form or by
any means, electronic, mechanical, photocopying, or otherwise
without the prior permission of the publisher.

ISBN 1 84172 795 4

KENT ARTS & LIBRARIES	
C152496881	
Bertrams	19.06.05
	£12.99

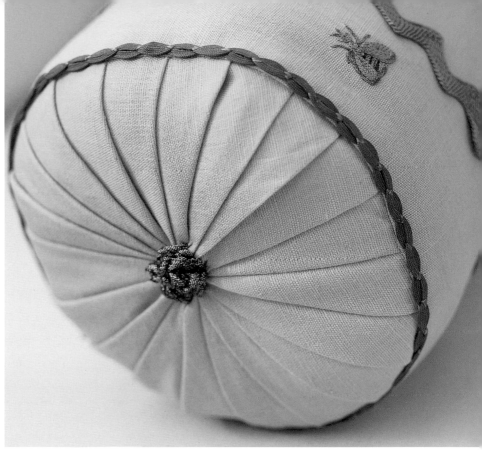

Contents

introduction 6

shapes 10
the star 12
bee bolster 16
striped tufted mattress 20
bobbles in the round 24

use of fabrics 28
stripes into squares 30
ribbon weave 34
floppy-edged cushion 38
crazy velvet patchwork 42

borders and edgings 46
scallops and zigzags 48
box-pleated border 52
double ruffle taffeta 56
double-flanged border 60

trimmings and fastenings 64
rope-edged knotted cushion 66
fastened with tassels 70
the envelope cushion 74
all trimmed 78
checked linen with contrast ties 82
loose linen cover 86

surface decoration 90
initials in cross stitch 92
autumnal appliqué 96

equipment and techniques 100
directory of suppliers 106
credits 107
glossary 110
index 111
acknowledgements 112

A whole book about cushions? A bit one-track? Maybe, but I for one love to prop a tired back against a soft, comfortable cushion, I adore using two or three sublimely soft pillows for a relaxing Sunday read of the newspapers, and other more ebullient and energetic members of my family quite like to indulge in pillow fights with some of our cushions. Consequently we wear out cushions on a fairly regular basis and, sad as I am to see a frayed favourite bite the dust, it does open up possibilities for new ideas and new fabrics and trimmings. I keep a large box of cuttings of all my favourite fabrics and an even larger box of remnants, antique textiles and other bits and pieces, and I love to put ideas together and toss a fresh new cushion on the sofa.

Cushions not only serve the purpose of softening a seat or supporting a back, but can also act as a foil for colour in a room. A plain, neutral sofa or armchair can be altered dramatically by the addition of a few primary-coloured cushions, or else soft muted ones. A wooden bench can take on a new look and added comfort with a bolster. Cushions don't need to be plain squares of colour — be bold and try circles and other shapes, mix colours and patterns, embroider a little pillow with someone's initials as a present, or make a mattress pad cushion for a hard stool. The possibilities are endless and this book offers inspiration as well as solid instructions for making cushions yourself.

Katrin Cargill

shapes

Mention the word 'cushion' and what probably springs to mind is a typical square shape. Although there are some differently shaped cushions available ready-made, if you are prepared to hunt out more unusual forms of pad, or better still make up your own shaped pads by simply stuffing a casing you have sewn yourself, then you can create original cushions in any number of shapes.

this page clockwise from top right *A tailored boxed triangle emphasized by thin dark piping; a bobble fringe in a deeper contrasting colour livens up a plain fabric; a rugby-ball-shaped cushion with contrasting piping, constructed from four panels, looks ready to fly through the air; green plaid squares echo the square shape of this cushion, which has Turkish corners caught together with a darker green thin piping; a narrow bolster in a woven linen check; a heart outlined with a heavy chenille fringe.*
below *Box cubes made from brushed cotton look fun in a modern room.*
bottom *Square on squares: a woven checked linen and viscose fabric with a tightly gathered little ruffled edge.*
opposite *A mattress effect is created by deep buttoning right through to the back. Great for benches and hard stools.*
opposite below left *A rectangle of horizontal stripes in cotton outlined with a bottle-green wool bobble fringe.*
opposite below right *Star struck: this three-dimensional shape can provide the only pattern on a plain sofa or chair.*

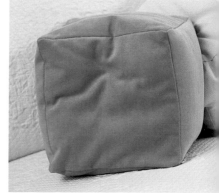

the star

This shape can really provide an unusual accent to a decorative scheme. It may not be one to curl up under for cozy reading, but a strongly contrasting coloured star or two can provide a wonderful focus in a room. It may be tricky to find this shape, but it is easy to make your own using a satisfyingly simple mathematical process. This one is made from a checked cotton with an embroidered floral motif, and is piped in a narrow contrasting colour for extra emphasis.

materials & equipment

120 cm (48 in) checked cotton, 115 cm (45 in) wide

contrasting fabric to make 250 cm (96 in) piping

250 cm (96 in) extra-thin piping cord, 3 mm (⅛ in) wide

kapok stuffing (or equivalent)

a sheet of paper 58 x 58 cm (23 x 23 in)

protractor

compass

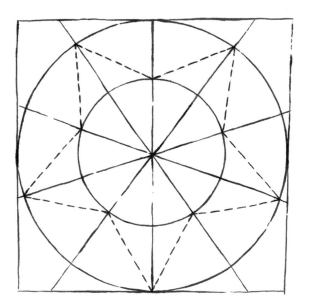

1 Make a star-shaped template on the paper by drawing a large circle with a 29 cm (11½ in) radius and a second smaller one inside it with a 16 cm (6½ in) radius. With a protractor and compass, mark off ten equidistant points around the outer circle, each exactly 36° apart. Using these marks and starting from the middle point, divide the square into ten sections. Use these reference points to draw an accurate five-point star. Cut out the star to use as a template.

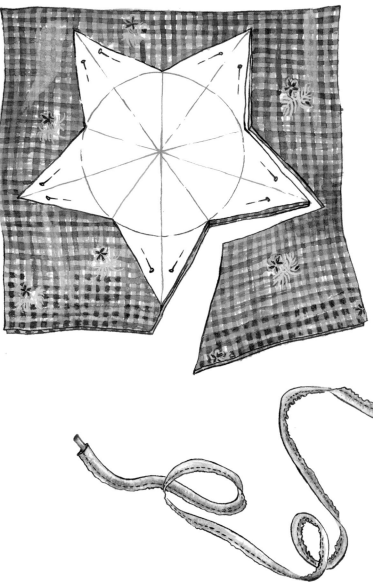

2 Cut out two 60 x 60 cm (24 x 24 in) squares of cotton. Lay them on top of one another and pin the template to the fabric through both layers. Cut around the template carefully, to cut two stars.

3 Using the contrasting fabric, make up 250 cm (96 in) of piping (see Techniques, page 103).

4 Place one star right side up and lay the piping around its edge, lining up the raw edges. Pin, baste and machine stitch in place using a 1 cm (½ in) seam allowance. To stitch the points of the star, work as close to the angle of each point as possible; leaving the needle in the fabric, lift the machine foot, swivel the fabric and then replace the foot. Begin stitching again following the edge of the star.

5 Place the second star over the piped one with right sides together, matching the raw edges. Pin, baste and machine stitch around the star edge, close to the piping, stitching between the piping and the raw edges. Sew a double row of stitches at each point of the star for reinforcement, but leave one section open for stuffing the cushion. Clip all the angles and points around the perimeter for a neater finish.

6 Turn the cushion cover right side out, press and then stuff it, being sure to push the stuffing right into the points (use the wrong end of a pencil or a blunt knitting needle for this).

7 When the stuffing is evenly distributed, with no lumps, close the open section neatly by hand using a slip stitch (see Techniques, page 101). Make sure the piping stays outside the line of stitches so that it will remain visible.

bee bolster

Bolster-shaped cushions are often associated with formal Empire furniture, but the shape can be used in a variety of situations: a metal daybed can be softened with a bolster, as can a particularly upright backed sofa or a rather firm chaise longue. The French use them as pillows on their beds, and little ones make jolly useful neck rests. This one is made from a bee motif fabric with beautifully pleated ends, and looks very stylish on a buttoned sofa.

materials & equipment

50 cm (20 in) embroidered bee fabric, 115 cm (45 in) wide

50 cm (20 in) plain fabric, 115 cm (45 in) wide

100 cm (40 in) thick decorative braid

75 cm (30 in) coordinating decorative braid

25 cm (10 in) a third braid

43 x 14 cm (17 x 5 ½ in) bolster pad

compass or string, pencil and pin

dressmaker's chalk

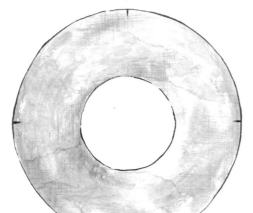

1 To make up the end pieces cut out two circles of plain fabric with a 42 cm (16½ in) diameter. Fold them in half and then quarters and mark these sections with dressmaker's chalk. Open each disc out again and draw a circle with a 13 cm (5 in) diameter in its centre. Fold into quarters and cut out the inner circle to form a ring.

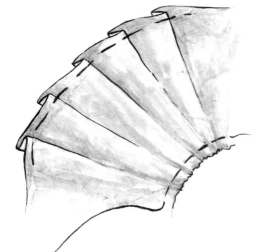

2 Measure and mark off points around the discs at intervals of 2.5 cm (1 in) followed by 2 cm (¾ in). Tuck each 2 cm (¾ in) fold under the 2.5 cm (1 in) section and pin and baste the pleats in place, 1 cm (½ in) from the outer circumference.

3 Now gather pleats around the inner ring to close up the centre gap and form two circles for the bolster ends. Secure the pleats tightly in position with basting stitches.

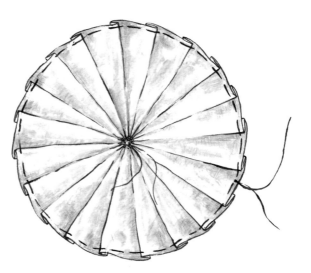

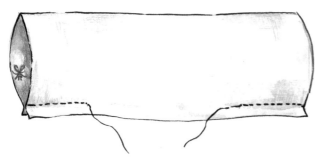

4 For the bolster tube, cut out one piece of bee embroidered fabric measuring 45 x 44 cm (18 x 17½ in). Fold it in half along the length, with right sides together, and machine stitch in from both ends of the longer edge for 10 cm (4 in) using a seam allowance of 1 cm (½ in).

5 To assemble the cover, with right sides together pin, baste and machine stitch the ends of the bolster to each of the pleated discs, using a 1 cm (½ in) seam allowance. Clip the curves around the edge to reduce the bulk.

6 Turn the cover out and press it, then insert the bolster pad. Slip stitch (see Techniques, page 101) the opening to a neat close.

7 To trim the bolster, hand sew the thick braid around both ends 5 cm (2 in) from the edge. Then hand sew the coordinating braid over the seam lines at each end.

8 To finish, twist two pieces of the third braid to form tight balls, and secure them with a few stitches. Hand sew in the middle of each end disc to hide the raw edges.

striped tufted mattress

Looking just like a mattress in miniature and made in heavy blue and cream linen, this functional squab is the ideal solution for softening wooden or metal seats. Because the casing is stuffed and the surface contours are made by hand tufting, you can make squabs of any size to make unyielding window seats or benches more comfortable.

materials & equipment

100 cm (40 in) blue-and-cream striped linen fabric, 115 cm (45 in) wide

enough stuffing to fill the 55 x 35 x 8 cm (22 x 14 x 3 in) finished cover

heavy linen thread

dressmaker's chalk

thick quilting needle

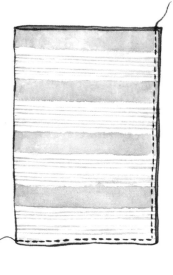

1   Cut out a piece of fabric measuring 88 x 65 cm (35 x 26 in). Fold the fabric in half lining up the shorter ends, with right sides together. Pin, baste and machine stitch the longer edge and one of the shorter ones, using a seam allowance of 1 cm (½ in).

2   To create the sides of the mattress, lay the fabric flat and at the closed end mark two matching points on both sides of the fabric; the points are 5 cm (2 in) from the raw edge of the shorter closed end, one is 4 cm (1½ in) from the folded long edge and the other is 5 cm (2 in) from the sewn long edge. Using dressmaker's chalk, mark a seam line on both sides of the fabric from both edges to each marked point, forming right angles.

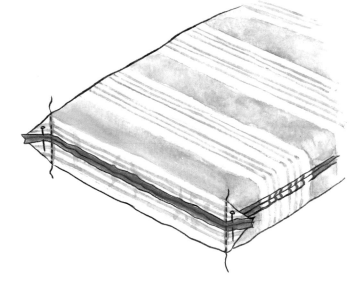

3   Take the corners of the chalk marks on either side of the fabric between thumb and forefinger and pull in opposite directions. The right angle seam lines will align and the side seams made in step 1 will open out. Pin and machine stitch between the aligned points in a straight line to give the cushion its 8 cm (3 in) depth. Repeat for the opposite corner.

4   Turn the cover right side out and insert the stuffing, taking care not to pack it in too tightly.

5   Fold in a 1 cm (½ in) seam allowance along one edge on the open end of the mattress and position it so that it overlaps the other raw edge. Neatly sew the top edge to the bottom edge together from corner to corner, using a slip stitch (see Techniques, page 101).

6 Tuck the ends of both pointed corners inside the body of the cushion so that you have two squared-up seams and the cushion is an equal width at both ends and an equal depth all round. Slip stitch the tucks to a neat close.

7 Using the heavy linen thread, make small stab stitches through the edge of the mattress, to form a border 1 cm (½ in) all the way round; gather up some of the filling in the border to create a padded effect. The stitches should be visible on both sides of the border. Repeat for the bottom edge.

8 To finish, cut twelve 2.5 cm (1 in) squares from the main fabric. Evenly space and mark the positions of six tufts on the top and bottom of the cushion, making sure they align. Using double linen thread and the quilting needle, sew one square on the bottom. Take the needle through to the other side and catch another square on the front. Secure it in place and double back through to the bottom of the cushion. Pull the thread tightly and knot it in place. Repeat this to secure the remaining tufts.

bobbles in the round

Circular pads are readily available, though they tend to be of the pancake variety. This pill-shaped size can lend itself to both traditional or modern situations. Here a creamy spotted muslin looks almost ethereal with the addition of two rows of cotton bobble fringe. This looks simpler to make than it is, so follow the steps carefully.

materials & equipment

150 cm (60 in) spotted muslin fabric, 150 cm (60 in) wide

250 cm (96 in) piping cord

250 cm (96 in) bobble fringe

38 cm (15 in) round cushion pad, 10 cm (4 in) deep

contrasting-coloured basting thread

1 For the top and bottom of the cushion cut out two circles of fabric, each with a 45 cm (18 in) diameter. For the side panel cut out a strip measuring 13 x 123 cm (5 x 49 in).

2 Place the side strip right side up. Cut the length of bobble fringe in half and pin and baste a length of bobble fringe along each of the outside edges of the side strip, matching the raw edges.

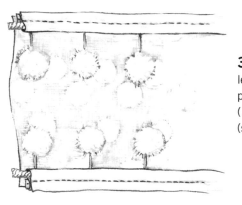

3 Next make the piping by cutting out the two lengths of fabric on the bias (see Techniques, page 103) each measuring 2.5 cm x 123 cm (1 x 49 in). Make up two lengths of piping (see Techniques, page 103).

4 Lay the piping over the bobble fringe so that the raw edges of the piping point away from the bobbles, which should lie towards the middle of the side strip. Pin, baste and machine stitch through all three layers. Repeat for the other long edge of the side strip.

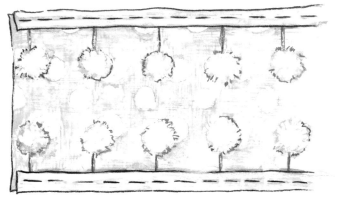

5 To join the open ends of the side strip, place the short ends right sides together and machine stitch with a 1 cm (½ in) seam allowance. Press open the seam. This completes the circular border.

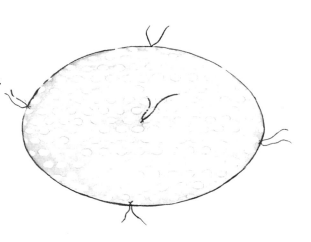

6 For the main body, fold each circle of fabric into quarters and mark the centre point with a contrasting-coloured stitch, then mark each quarter point on both the perimeters in the same way. Use the stitched markers to mark off quarter points on both the top and bottom edges of the circular border.

7 To gather the top and bottom of the cushion, first make a small circle of running stitches, about 4 cm (1½ in) in diameter, in the centre of each round section. Do not yet pull into a gather. Then make a circle of running stitches around the perimeter 1 cm (½ in) in from the outside edge. Pull in all the gathers in turn so that both round pieces fit within the circular border and the marker points line up.

8 To cover the gathered middles hand sew a bobble or a button in place on both sides of the cushion.

9 To join the cushion together turn all three pieces to the wrong side. With right sides together and matching all the marks on the perimeters, pin, baste and machine stitch the top of the cushion to the border leaving a 1 cm (½ in) seam allowance. Repeat for the bottom, but leave an opening of 30 cm (12 in).

10 Turn right side out, insert cushion pad and slip stitch (see Techniques, page 101) closed.

use of fabrics

Fabric is available in a bewildering array. However, if you think beyond the three basic elements of any fabric — colour, pattern and texture — you will see that there are all sorts of ways you can play with these elements for decorative effect. By piecing together clever contrasts and combinations of fabrics you can achieve spectacular results.

clockwise from top right *An exquisitely delicate cut velvet and chenille tassel dangles on the corner of a woven organdie ribbon cushion; the regal-looking crest on this impressive cushion is sewn directly onto the front and is set off by the rich gold metallic piping with looped corners; rich woven damask needs only the adornment of a thin rope border; a cotton and gaufraged velvet stripe looks smart with chenille fringing; the pattern of this fabric emphasizes the long bolster shape; a white woollen bobble fringe trims a strong animal print.*
below *Gaufraged golden thistles on a wine-coloured velvet, edged in two-tone rope and tassels.*
bottom *Jewel-coloured wool and mohair to keep you warm.*
opposite above right *A patchwork of rich and sumptuous silks, separated by a golden metallic ribbon, edged in a multicoloured tasselled fringe.*
opposite above far right *This lovely antique needlepoint cushion is trimmed with golden ribbon and a tasslled fringe.*
opposite *A harlequin velvet cushion and a knife-edged golden cotton damask one.*

stripes into squares

A cushion to add a touch of imperial style to a daybed or sofa. Link the material and tassel to other colour themes in the room, or perhaps let it stand alone to make a bold statement in what might otherwise be a somewhat dull corner. Here construction and design rely on four triangles mitred together into a square.

materials & equipment

125 cm (50 in) striped cotton, 115 cm (45 in) wide

70 cm (28 in) thick piping cord

decorative tassel

45 cm (18 in) cushion pad

straight-edged ruler

1 For the front of the cushion cut out four pieces of fabric into identical triangles, each 46 x 32.5 x 32.5 cm (18½ x 13¼ x 13¼ in), which includes a 1 cm (½ in) seam allowance.

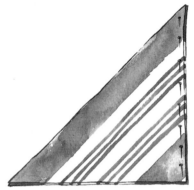

2 Place two of the triangles right sides together. Carefully align the stripes and pin, baste and machine stitch along a 1 cm (½ in) seam. Repeat for the other two triangles. Open out and press open the seams.

3 Place the two seamed triangles right sides together. Carefully align the stripes and pin, baste and machine stitch together along the straight edge. Press open the adjoining seams.

4 For the back, cut out a piece of fabric that is 15 cm (6 in) wider than the 45 cm (18 in) cushion, and 25 cm (10 in) longer. Fold in half, press and cut into two pieces.

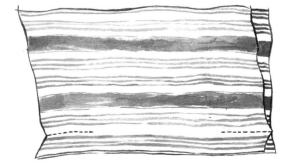

5 Lay the two pieces right sides together. Pin, baste and machine stitch a seam along one of the long sides 5 cm (2 in) from the edge, leaving a 35 cm (14 in) gap in the middle. Press open.

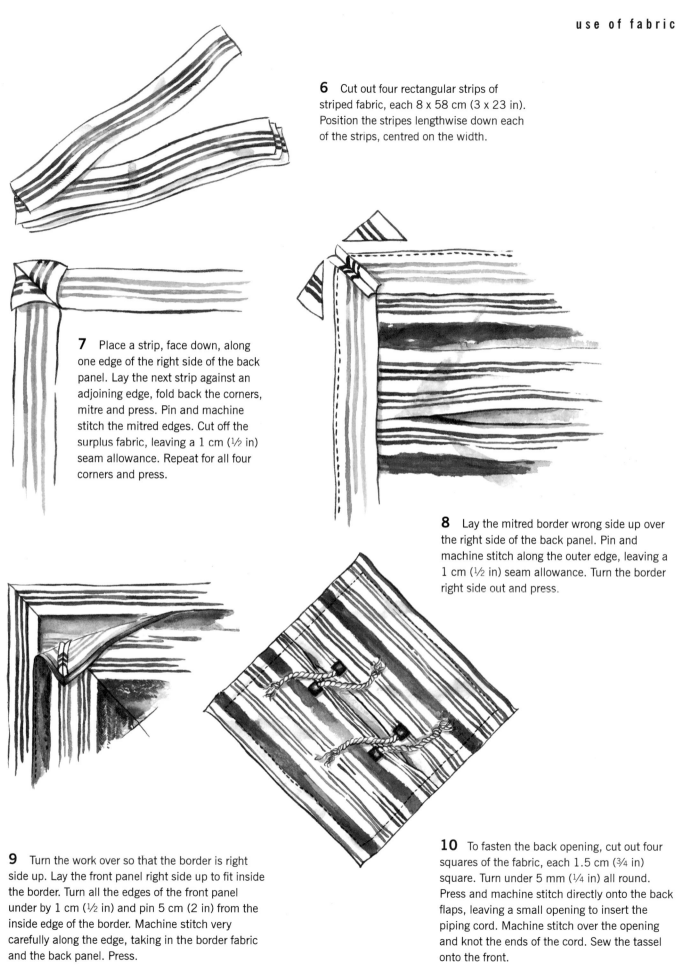

6 Cut out four rectangular strips of striped fabric, each 8 x 58 cm (3 x 23 in). Position the stripes lengthwise down each of the strips, centred on the width.

7 Place a strip, face down, along one edge of the right side of the back panel. Lay the next strip against an adjoining edge, fold back the corners, mitre and press. Pin and machine stitch the mitred edges. Cut off the surplus fabric, leaving a 1 cm (½ in) seam allowance. Repeat for all four corners and press.

8 Lay the mitred border wrong side up over the right side of the back panel. Pin and machine stitch along the outer edge, leaving a 1 cm (½ in) seam allowance. Turn the border right side out and press.

9 Turn the work over so that the border is right side up. Lay the front panel right side up to fit inside the border. Turn all the edges of the front panel under by 1 cm (½ in) and pin 5 cm (2 in) from the inside edge of the border. Machine stitch very carefully along the edge, taking in the border fabric and the back panel. Press.

10 To fasten the back opening, cut out four squares of the fabric, each 1.5 cm (¾ in) square. Turn under 5 mm (¼ in) all round. Press and machine stitch directly onto the back flaps, leaving a small opening to insert the piping cord. Machine stitch over the opening and knot the ends of the cord. Sew the tassel onto the front.

ribbon weave

This sumptuous woven ribbon cushion works on the simple principle of basket weaving. Seven different shades of velvet ribbon are cut into strips of equal length and woven across the surface of the cushion. This idea can be adapted using just two or three colours for a draughtboard effect or even just one colour to show off the weave. The velvet tassels on the corners add the perfect finishing touch.

materials & equipment

50 cm (20 in) velvet fabric, 115 cm (45 in) wide

50 cm (20 in) thin interlining fabric

*seven different colours of velvet ribbon, 2.5 cm (1 in) wide,
with a total length of 18m (60 ft)*

200 cm (78 in) velvet piping

four tassels

45 cm (18 in) square cushion pad

45 cm (18 in) zip

1 To create the ribbon effect on the front cut 48 cm (19½ in) strips from each colour of ribbon. It does not matter if there are more strips of some colours – this will add to the effect. Cut out a piece of interlining fabric 48 cm (19 in) square.

2 Pin the strips face up along one edge of the interlining, leaving a 1 cm (½ in) gap at each side. Try to achieve a random effect with the colours. Baste and machine stitch along the top of the ribbons to secure them, allowing 1 cm (½ in) for the seam allowance.

3 Starting from the top, weave the remaining ribbons horizontally, threading them under and over the vertical ribbons. Alternate the colours to create a random pattern and anchor them to the sides with pins. Push each ribbon tightly against the one above.

4 Continue interweaving the ribbons until the interlining is covered and then baste the three loose sides down.

5 For the back, cut out two pieces of velvet measuring 48 x 25 cm (19½ x 10 in). Place the panels right sides together and along one of the longer sides machine stitch in from the edge for 5 cm (2 in) on each side; use a seam allowance of 2.5 cm (1 in). Open out the seams and press.

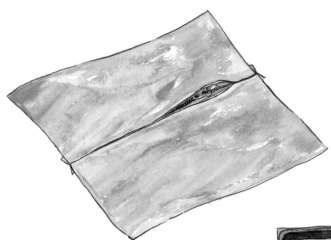

6 Lay the closed zip underneath the opening, right side up and between the two seams, making sure that the fabric actually meets over the middle of the zip. Pin, baste and machine stitch down both sides of the zip to secure it in place.

7 Lay the velvet piping around the perimeter of the back piece on the right side, lining up the raw edges. Pin and baste them together.

8 With right sides facing position the front section over the piped back panel, making sure the zip is open. Pin, baste and machine stitch through all the layers as close to the piping as possible. Clip the corners and trim and finish the raw edges to prevent fraying (see Techniques, page 102).

9 Turn the cover right side out, insert the cushion pad and fasten the zip. Attach a tassel to each corner with small hand stitches.

floppy-edged cushion

Stone-washed silk has an irresistible texture. Here muted blue and purple silk are pieced together to form a striped pattern. The deep full flaps that make up the border, combined with the texture of the fabric, give this cushion a wonderfully floppy and extravagant feel that will add a touch of sheer luxury to a room.

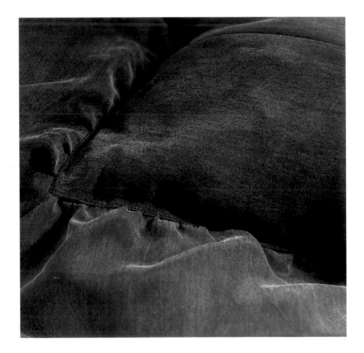

materials & equipment

100 cm (40 in) purple stone-washed silk, 115 cm (45 in) wide

75 cm (30 in) blue stone-washed silk, 115 cm (45 in) wide

45 cm (18 in) square cushion pad

1 For the back, cut out two pieces of purple silk, each measuring 48 x 30 cm (19 x 12 in). Turn under a double 5 mm (¼ in) hem along one of the longer edges on both pieces and pin, baste and machine stitch it in place.

2 Overlap the hemmed edges of each panel by 10 cm (4 in) and pin and baste along both side edges of the overlap. The back should now measure 48 x 48 cm (19 x 19 in) with a deep flap for inserting the cushion and closing the cover.

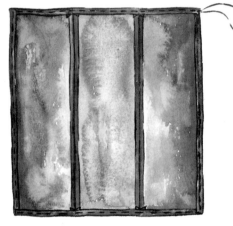

3 For the front, cut out two panels of purple silk, each measuring 16 x 48 cm (6½ x 19 in) and one panel of blue silk measuring 19 x 48 cm (8 x 19 in).

4 Place the three panels side by side matching the long edges, with the blue panel in the middle. With right sides facing pin, baste and machine stitch the blue silk to one side of each of the purple pieces, using a seam allowance of 1 cm (½ in). Turn under a 1 cm (½ in) seam allowance on all four sides and baste it in place. This is the front panel.

5 For the border flaps, cut two strips 23 x 82 cm (9 x 33 in) from each colour of silk fabric. Fold the strips in half down the length with the right side out and press to mark the fold line.

6 Open out the strips wrong side up. Fold each end into a mitre by turning back the corners and press. Cut along the fold line to form triangular points.

7 Place the strips corner to corner, with alternate colours touching. With right sides facing pin, baste and machine stitch the mitred corners together using a seam allowance of 1 cm (½ in).

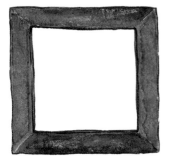

8 Turn the completed deep flap border right side out and press along the fold line on each strip to form a square.

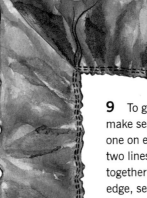

9 To gather the deep flap border, make separate rows of gathers, one on each raw edge. Hand sew two lines of running stitches close together 1 cm (½ in) in from each edge, sewing through the two layers. Gently pull all of the rows of gathers in turn until each inner edge measures 48 cm (19 in).

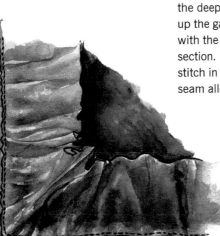

10 Take the back panel and lay it flat with the right side up. Place the deep flap border over it, lining up the gathered edges of the flap with the raw edges of the back section. Pin, baste and machine stitch in place using a 1 cm (½ in) seam allowance.

11 Press the deep flap border outwards, then turn the work over and press the narrow seam allowances around all four sides towards the middle.

12 With the right side up, place the front panel over the wrong side of the back panel, lining up the turned-in edges on the front with the stitching line around the edge of the back. Pin and baste the two pieces together and join them with a tight 5 mm (¼ in) zigzag stitch, stitching right against the edge of the front panel. Alternatively, use top stitch.

13 Press the cushion cover and insert the pad through the deep flap at the back. Pull the flap closed so that the pad is completely covered.

crazy velvet patchwork

The age-old craft of patchwork has enduring appeal. Here a puzzle of velvet offcuts, some slightly bald and worn, have been pieced together in a random fashion and the joins disguised with decorative feather stitching in a strong colour. This idea would work equally well with a selection of old silk offcuts.

materials & equipment

assorted colours of velvet to cover the 40 x 45 cm (16 x 18 in) front section

50 cm (20 in) velvet, 115 cm (45 in) wide for the back

200 cm (78 in) rope edging

stranded embroidery cotton in a contrasting colour

40 x 45 cm (16 x 18 in) cushion pad

one sheet each of drawing paper, tracing paper and thick paper

embroidery needle

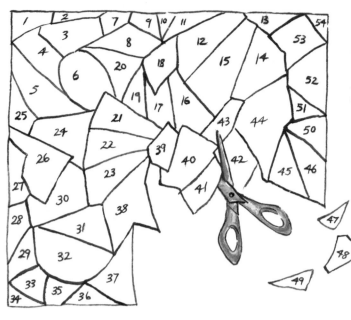

1 To make up the front, sketch an arrangement of crazy-shaped pieces on a sheet of paper 40 x 45 cm (16 x 18 in). Trace off the design onto thicker paper and give each segment a number before cutting out each shape, then mark the same number on the back.

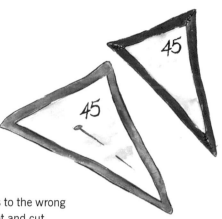

2 Pin the front face of the shapes to the wrong side of the different colours of velvet and cut them out, adding a 5 mm (¼ in) seam allowance to the fabric around all sides.

3 Turn in the seam allowance on each piece. Press and secure it in place at the corners with a few small stitches.

4 Now reconstruct the puzzle design over the original drawing, matching up the numbers segment by segment. Working from the top downwards join the shapes together using a slip stitch (see Techniques, page 101), removing the templates as you join each piece.

5 Once the front section is in one piece, sew over all the seam lines using a feather embroidery stitch (see Techniques, page 101).

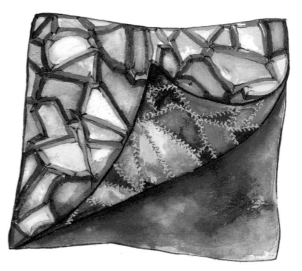

6 For the back, cut out a 42 x 48 cm (17 x 19 in) piece of velvet. Finish the raw edges (see Techniques, page 102), turn in a 1 cm (½ in) seam allowance on the wrong side and press in place. Lay the front and back sections right sides together.

7 Hand sew the front and back sections together along three of the sides using an overcasting stitch.

8 Turn the cover right side out and insert the cushion pad. Slip stitch the opening to a neat close leaving a small gap to insert the end of the rope edging.

9 Cut the rope edging to fit the perimeter of the cushion and hand sew it around the edges, feeding the end of the rope into the small gap before sewing it down for a neat finish.

borders and edgings

By emphasizing the outline of a cushion you can turn a bland accessory that fades into the background into something that really gets noticed. Borders come in all shapes and forms — from the subtlest piping to more dramatic frills or flaps, edgings are integral to the design.

left *Two cushions made from antique woven linen: one has a pillowcase flap with covered buttons for closure; the other has a deeper top-closing flap, which uses the same fabric at right angles, with hand-sewn buttonholes.*
bottom left to right *A deep quilted border has been stitched with heavy linen thread on plain red linen fabric. A white cotton triangle has a tightly ruffled border of wired hessian ribbon in a contrasting khaki. Antique striped woven linen has been mitred to form a pattern and finished with smart red piping.*
opposite right and far right *These soft and comfy fleece cushions have been blanket-stitched around the edges in contrasting colours. A fresh country weave has a coordinating lightly gathered frill, used as a single layer with a tiny hem.*
opposite below from left to right
A tightly gathered border is made from strips of plain red fabric, gathered onto a thick piping cord. Linen tea towels come out of the kitchen to make excellent cushions, their borders providing a natural flap to stitch around. An elegant wavy flap is edged in a narrow bias binding in a contrasting red, to provide a tailored finish that emphasizes the curves.

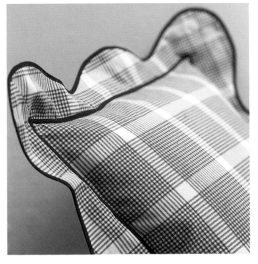

left to right *A linen damask cushion has an outer casing of the finest silk organza with a deeply frilled edge — the ultimate luxury. A thin plain linen cushion with a ruffled edge, outlined in the palest blue bias binding. Twisted rope borders a smart tailored linen stripe.*

scallops and zigzags

There is a timeless magic in scallops and zigzags, a well-known decorative device for fabrics. These natural linens in neutral beige and white look fresh and modern, and can be applied to most shapes and sizes to great effect. The instructions here are for scallops but the same technique can be used to create a lovely zigzag.

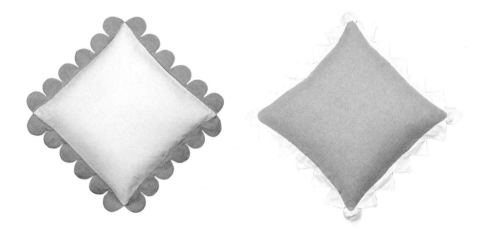

materials & equipment

50 cm (20 in) beige linen, 115 cm (45 in) wide

50 cm (20 in) white linen, 115 cm (45 in) wide

45 cm (18 in) square pad

compass or circular template

ruler

1 To make the scallops, cut out four strips of beige fabric 48 x 17 cm (19 x 7 in). Fold them in half lengthways with right sides facing and press.

2 Using a circular template or a compass draw six circles on the strip, each with a 7 cm (2½ in) diameter. Position the line of circles so there is a 5 mm (½ in) gap at each open end, a 16 mm (⅝ in) gap in between each circle and a 2.5 cm (1 in) gap between the bottom of each circle and the raw edge. Draw a straight line through the middle of all six circles. To create the scallops, follow the outline of the top half of each circle and extend the outline 5 mm (¼ in) below the line linking the half circles together.

3 Machine stitch along the line of scallops on all four strips and cut out.

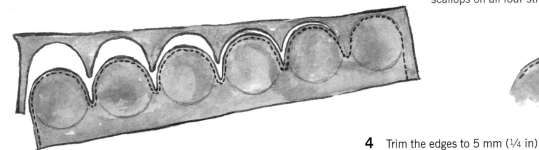

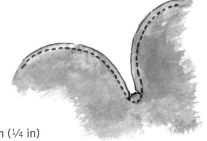

4 Trim the edges to 5 mm (¼ in) and snip in between the scallops. Turn right side out, pushing the scallops into shape, and press.

5 For the front of the cushion cut out a piece of white fabric measuring 48 cm (19 in) square. For the back, cut out two pieces of white fabric, each measuring 48 x 29 cm (19 x 11½ in).

6 To make the back, lay the two pieces right sides together. Machine stitch 8 cm (3 in) in from each side along the longer edge, with a 5 cm (2 in) seam allowance.

7 Turn the back panel wrong side up and open out the seam allowance. On each seam allowance turn under 1 cm (½ in) and machine stitch a hem close to the raw edge.

8 Machine stitch the open hemmed seam allowance of the top piece to the main body of the same piece on the right side of the fabric, starting 8 cm (3 in) in from each side and 3 cm (1¼ in) above the central fold.

9 Now press the back panel with both seam allowances pointing towards the top piece.

10 Lay the back panel right side up and machine two narrow, parallel rows of vertical stitching extending for 3 cm (1¼ in) from the central fold and beginning 8 cm (3 in) from the sides, thus securing the flap.

11 To make the ties, cut out two strips of white fabric measuring 2 x 30 cm (¾ x 12 in). Hem the long sides of each strip, and press. Attach one tie to the middle of each side of the back opening by machine stitching across its width 3 cm (1¼ in) from the central fold. Finish the ends of the ties by cutting them on the diagonal.

12 Next place the four scalloped borders along each edge of the right side of the front piece, lining up the raw edges and leaving a 1 cm (½ in) gap at each end. Pin, baste and machine stitch down each side.

13 Place the finished back piece over the front piece, with right sides facing. Pin, baste and machine stitch the front to the back with a 1 cm (½ in) seam allowance, being careful to stitch just inside the seam attaching the scallops to the front piece. Finish the raw edges (see Techniques, page 102) and clip the corners. Turn the casing right side out and press. Then insert the cushion and fasten the ties.

box-pleated border

Box pleats make a very smart and tailored edging to a cushion. Although they require quite a bit of fabric, they are simple to make and most effective. Stripes lend themselves particularly well to this technique, though care needs to be taken to keep them in line. On this cushion, the narrow stripe appears only on the front of the pleats.

materials & equipment

50 cm (20 in) cotton motif main fabric, 115 cm (45 in) wide

50 cm (20 in) cotton fabric with alternate panels of 9 cm (3 ½ in) wide stripes

25 x 40 cm (10 x 16 in) cushion pad

1 Cut two pieces 27 x 42 cm (11 x 17 in) from the main fabric, with a motif centred on one piece. For the border, cut out a 18 x 278 cm (7 x 113 in) strip from the striped fabric, joining lengths where needed.

2 Take the border strip and stitch the short ends together with right sides facing and stripes matching, then press the seam open. Fold the completed circle in half lengthways with wrong sides facing and press the fold line.

3 To make a box pleat, fold the plain section 2.5 cm (1 in) into itself on both sides so that the narrow stripes come together over the top of it. Pin the pleat in place on the raw edge and repeat all the way along the strip. Baste the pleats in position using a seam allowance of 1 cm (½ in) and press.

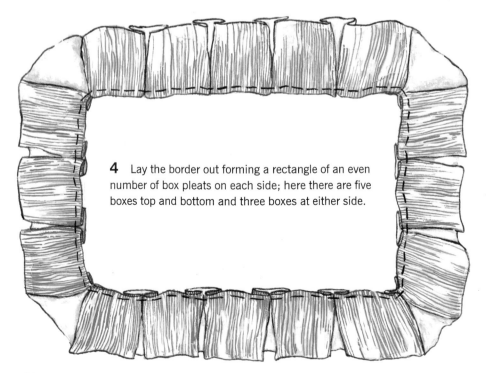

4 Lay the border out forming a rectangle of an even number of box pleats on each side; here there are five boxes top and bottom and three boxes at either side.

5 Snip into the raw edges of the fabric almost as far as the seam allowance on the corner pleats. Take the panel with the centred motif, which is the front panel, and lay it right side up. Lay the border over it with the large striped pleats facing down. Match the corners and line up the raw edges, then pin and baste the border to the panel, using a 1 cm (½ in) seam allowance.

6 Now take the back panel and place it over the bordered front piece, right side down and lining up the four sides. Pin, baste and machine stitch around three sides of the cover and turn it right side out.

7 Insert the cushion pad and slip stitch (see Techniques, page 101) the opening on the back of the cushion to a neat close.

double ruffle taffeta

Silk taffeta has a magical quality to it, and no better way to see it than when it is gathered and bunched. Here a tiny checked taffeta is used with a double ruffle effect. The outside ruffle is a single layer of fabric, and the smaller inside one uses the fabric doubled and tightly gathered, to make a specially sumptuous cushion.

materials & equipment

150 cm (60 in) checked taffeta, 115 cm (45 in) wide

45 cm (18 in) square cushion pad

38 cm (15 in) zip

1   For the front, cut out one piece of fabric measuring 48 x 48 cm (19 x 19 in). For the back, cut out two pieces measuring 48 x 25 cm (19 x 10 in). For the ruffle, cut out two strips, each measuring 10 cm x 400 cm (4 x 160 in), joining lengths where necessary.

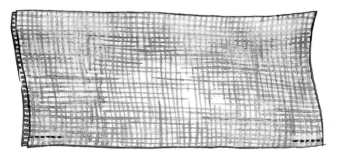

2   To make up the back, place the two panels right sides together and along one of the longer sides machine stitch for 5 cm (2 in) in from the edge on either side, leaving a seam allowance of 2.5 cm (1 in). Open out the seams and press.

3   Turn the back panel over to the right side and lay the closed zip underneath the opening, right side up and between the two seams, making sure that the fabric actually meets over the middle of the zip. Pin, baste and machine stitch down either side of the zip using the zip foot if you have one. Make sure the zip is open before you continue sewing.

4   To make the border, with right sides facing stitch the short ends of one of the ruffle strips to form one piece. Repeat for the other strip and press the seams open. Neatly hem one of the strips by turning in 5 mm (¼ in) and machine stitch all the way around.

5   Fold the other strip in half, wrong sides facing, but do not press the fold. Place the folded strip alongside the right side of the hemmed one and line up the raw edges; baste all the way round, 1 cm (½ in) from the edge.

6 Sew a double row of running stitches and pull the thread into even gathers until the ruffle measures 180 cm (72 in).

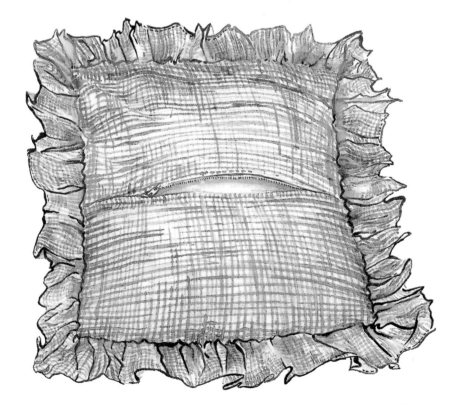

7 Lay the front piece right side up and place the double ruffle right side down along all four sides, lining up the raw edges. Pin and baste the border in place 1 cm (½ in) from the outside edge.

8 Place the back and the front pieces right sides together, pin, baste and machine stitch all round the edge with a 1 cm (½ in) seam allowance, being careful to stitch inside the gathering stitches. At each corner work the stitches in a curve and not a sharp right angle. Trim the edges and clip the corners. Turn the cover out through the open zip and insert the cushion.

double-flanged border

Two sophisticated woven silk patterns look very stylish with double layers of flanges that give a glimpse of the contrasting fabric. The texture of the silk lends itself particularly well to this style, which is simple enough to work just as well in a stronger pattern. The cushion is deceptively easy to make, and has a modern feel to it.

materials & equipment

75 cm (30 in) figured silk, 150 cm (60 in) wide

75 cm (30 in) plain silk, 150 cm (60 in) wide

45 cm (18 in) square cushion pad

1 Cut four pieces of silk measuring 60 x 60 cm (24 x 24 in), two each from both fabrics. Ensure that the grain runs straight and not diagonally, and that the pattern falls neatly.

2 Lay two pieces of the same fabric right sides facing and pin, baste and machine stitch them together 1 cm (½ in) from the edge all the way round, but leaving a 10 cm (4 in) opening on one side. Repeat for the other fabric.

3 Turn the fabric right side out and slip stitch (see Techniques, page 101) the opening to a neat close. Press. Repeat this process for the other piece of silk.

4 Take each separate panel and pin, baste and machine stitch a line along one edge only, 6 cm (2½ in) in from the edge and 6 cm (2½ in) in from the sides.

5 Place the two panels over each other, lining up the two edges showing a line of stitching. Pin, baste and machine stitch the three remaining sides through all layers, so forming a 6 cm (2½ in) flap all round.

6 Insert the cushion pad and close the cover inside the two open flaps by hand, using a slip stitch and following the line of machine stitches.

7 To neaten the corners of the flap, oversew the four points with a few small hand stitches.

For a richer and more colourful effect, make up the inside of each panel in a third shade of silk, which will be revealed when the flaps open out.

trimmings and fastenings

Unadorned, a cushion tends to blend into the seating or surface it is placed upon. To make a feature of the cushion itself calls for some clever ideas to dress up the basic shape. Choose from the wealth of decorative trimmings and fastenings available to embellish cushions in dozens of ways.

below *Three examples of back fastening ties: finished with knots; secured by square tabs of the fabric; doubled cotton with zigzagged edges.*
centre *Three rows of a deep natural cotton fringe cover the surface of cream cotton to make a funky cushion.*
bottom left *A striped silk cushion has a doubled ruffled edge, finished with a pleated satin ribbon.*
bottom right *For a neat finish on this plaid cushion, the fan edging has been box-pleated at each of the corners.*

above left and right *Two rectangles: one has a ruched fringe to contrast with the subtle plaid; the other is finished in a two-tone fan edging with four tufted linen buttons sewn down each side.*
above centre *A finely woven pure white linen cushion has a surface-applied fringe made of natural hemp-like string.*
clockwise from top right *Buttons and tufts: silk looped button; deep tufted linen; a wonderful antique hand-sewn button; a tuft made from cutting a square piece of fabric with pinking shears. The diamond shape and the circular patchwork detail are outlined by rows of tiny bobble fringe in a dark purple. A crewel work cushion is trimmed in a dark green linen fringe.*

rope-edged knotted cushion

A cool Indian madras cotton is paired with a bright red rope border, sewn directly onto the edge of the cushion. The extended corners are long enough to be knotted, to create a fresh and different look. A pile of cushions in inexpensive contrasting Madras fabrics can look gloriously exuberant.

materials & equipment

200 cm (78 in) cotton fabric, 115 cm (45 in) wide

500 cm (192 in) rope edging

45 cm (18 in) square cushion pad

100 cm (40 in) square piece of pattern paper

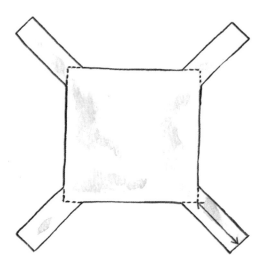

1   Make up a paper pattern in the shape of the template shown; the main panel of the cushion measures 48 cm (19 in) square and at each corner there is an extension or 'tail' 25 cm (10 in) long and 8 cm (3 in) wide.

2   Fold the fabric in half, right sides together, matching raw edges. Place the paper pattern on the fabric and pin it in place. Cut out two pieces.

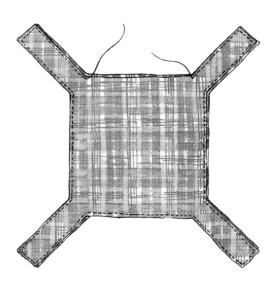

3   Remove the paper pattern and pin, baste and machine stitch all round the edge of the panel and the tails using a 1 cm (½ in) seam allowance. Leave one side of the panel open to insert the cushion. Trim the corners and turn the tails inside out as you machine, pushing out the corners with a blunt pencil or knitting needle.

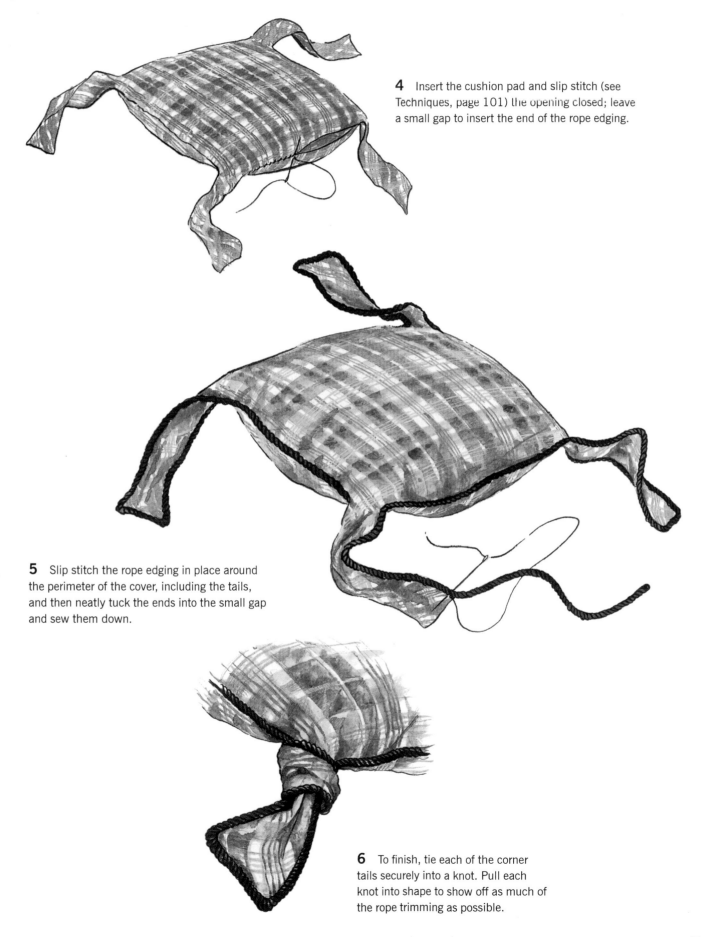

4   Insert the cushion pad and slip stitch (see Techniques, page 101) the opening closed; leave a small gap to insert the end of the rope edging.

5   Slip stitch the rope edging in place around the perimeter of the cover, including the tails, and then neatly tuck the ends into the small gap and sew them down.

6   To finish, tie each of the corner tails securely into a knot. Pull each knot into shape to show off as much of the rope trimming as possible.

fastened with tassels

In this formal design, cream linen encases a silk inner lining to create a sleek and sophisticated cushion. These luxurious fabrics are appropriately dressed up with a pair of silk tassels that provide an elegant means of fastening, and the open end of the linen casing is delicately edged with drawn thread work.

materials & equipment

50 cm (20 in) cream evenly woven linen, 115 cm (45 in) wide

85 cm (34 in) striped silk, 115 cm (45 in) wide

two silk tassels

40 cm (16 in) square cushion pad

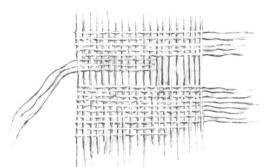

1 For the outer casing, cut out one piece of linen measuring 48 x 92 cm (19 x 37 in). To decorate the top border make a line of drawn thread work. Begin by drawing out five threads, 8 cm (3 in) in from one of the longer sides.

2 On the same long edge, turn under twice a 2.5 cm (1 in) hem. Align the folded edge neatly close to the line of drawn threads and press. Baste this fold down.

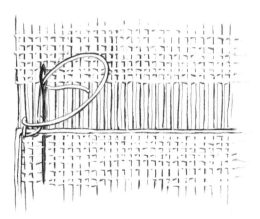

3 Secure your thread at one end of the hem, then pass the needle under three threads, pulling them into a bundle. Sew a small vertical stitch through the right side, coming out through the turned hem, to the right of the thread bundle. Continue this pattern for the length of the hem.

4 Turn the fabric upside down and repeat this stitching on the opposite edge, working from left to right and taking the same threads in each bundle as those taken opposite. The result will be a ladder pattern.

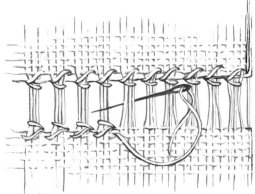

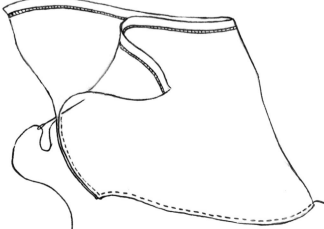

5 Make up the casing by folding it in half across the width, right sides together and lining up the edges. Pin, baste and machine stitch around the two undecorated sides, using a 1 cm (½ in) seam allowance.

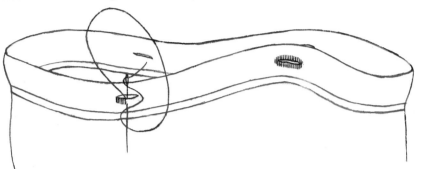

6 Finish the seam (see Techniques, page 102) and press it to one side then sew it down along the hemmed border. Turn the cover right side out and press.

7 To complete the casing, make four buttonholes to fit the tassels along the open edge. Cut two slits through all layers on each side, making sure that they are even and opposite, and finish the raw edge with a buttonhole stitch (see Techniques, page 102).

8 For the inner cushion, cut one piece of silk fabric 43 x 82 cm (17 x 33 in). Fold it in half across the width with right sides facing and pin, baste and machine stitch along two sides, using a seam allowance of 1 cm (½ in).

9 Turn the cover right side out, press and insert the cushion pad. Close up the open side using a slip stitch (see Techniques, page 101).

10 Place the completed inner silk cushion inside the outer linen casing with the folded edge at the top and attach the tassels for a decorative fastening.

the envelope cushion

Tassels offer a quick and easy way to add a touch of style and they are available ready-made in all shapes and textures — from coarse rope to the softest silk. Here a neutral linen is trimmed with piping and a silk tassel appears to close the 'envelope' flap for a cushion with a simple, understated elegance.

materials & equipment

100 cm (40 in) linen fabric, 115 cm (45 in) wide

300 cm (120 in) piping cord

one button

one tassel with a looped fastening

45 cm (18 in) square cushion pad

1 To make up the cushion cut out two pieces of fabric 48 x 48 cm (19 x 19 in) and two triangular shapes with a 48 cm (19 in) base and 40 cm (16 in) sides, for the flap. For the piped edge cut out 4 cm (1½ in) wide strips on the bias to make up 300 cm (120 in) of piping (see Techniques, page 103).

2 Begin by trimming the flap. Lay a section of piping along the two 40 cm (16 in) sides of one of the triangular pieces, right side up. Pin, baste and machine stitch it in place.

3 Lay the second triangle over the piped one, right side down and pin, baste and machine stitch them together close to the piping cord. Clip the point of the triangle, turn the sewn flap right side out and press.

4 Pin, baste and machine stitch the raw edge of the flap to the right side of one of the edges of the front piece, using a seam allowance of 1 cm (½ in).

5 With the front piece still right side up, lay the piping all round the four raw edges, going over the top of the flap. Pin, baste and machine stitch the piping to the front, keeping the stitches close to the cord and inside the row of stitching on the flap.

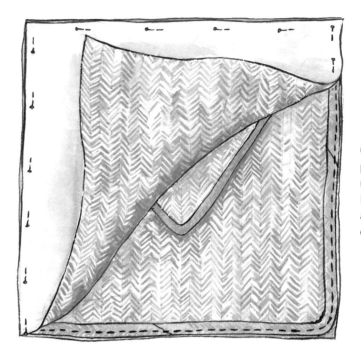

6 Place the back panel over the top of the front piece with right sides facing and pin, baste and machine stitch them together along three sides, leaving the bottom edge open and using a seam allowance of 1 cm (½ in). Clip the corners, turn the cover right side out and press.

7 Hand sew the button to the front of the cushion at the point of the triangular flap, securing the flap to the cushion. Insert the cushion pad and sew up the opening to a neat close using a slip stitch (see Techniques, page 101), but be careful that the piped edge is visible on the outside.

8 Add a decorative touch by attaching a looped tassel around the button. Secure it with a few hand stitches through the loop.

all trimmed

Rich colours and textures contrast to make a very sumptuous cushion. Spinach-green linen forms the basis with a wide flap that is edged in thin red velvet piping on the outside, and rich red wool fringing on the inside. The Tyrolean floral trimming has been sewn onto a wide cotton binding to show up the colours better. This design lends itself to a variety of different combinations of colours and trimmings.

materials & equipment

100 cm (40 in) heavyweight spinach-green linen, 115 cm (45 in) wide

200 cm (80 in) burgundy fringe

275 cm (110 in) narrow bright red velvet piping

175 cm (70 in) red tape, 2.5 cm (1 in) wide

175 cm (70 in) decorative braid

45 cm (18 in) square cushion pad

two green buttons to match main fabric

1 For the front, cut out a piece of main fabric measuring 48 x 48 cm (19 x 19 in). For the back, cut out two pieces of main fabric, each measuring 58 x 32 cm (23 x 12½ in). For the border, cut out four pieces of main fabric, each measuring 7.5 x 58 cm (3 x 23 in).

2 To make the back, finish both the long edges of both back panels to prevent fraying (see Techniques, page 102).

3 Lay the two back panels right sides together and pin, baste and machine a line of stitches 9 cm (3½ in) in from the side edges and 2.5 cm (1 in) above one of the long edges. Then turn the fabric 90° and continue sewing a vertical line down to the same finished edge.

4 Open out the back panel and press the two seam allowances in the same direction.

5 For the border, take one strip and place it right side down along one edge of the back panel. Fold the corner of the strip in at a 45° angle. Lay the next strip, fold the corner into a mitre and press. Repeat so that all four strips are neatly mitred.

6 Remove the strips and machine stitch along each pressed fold to join the strips into a border. Snip off the excess fabric to a 1 cm (½ in) seam allowance.

7 Now attach the piping to the back panel. Lay the back panel flat, right side up. Pin and baste the velvet piping around the perimeter of the back panel, matching the raw edges and leaving a 1 cm (½ in) seam allowance all round.

8 Lay the mitred border over the back panel (with piping now attached) right sides together. Pin, baste and machine stitch together, working the stitches between the piping and the raw edges, leaving a 1 cm (½ in) seam allowance. Turn right side out and press.

9 With the back of the cushion right side down and the attached mitred border right side up baste the inside edges of the border to the back panel to hold it in place. Take the length of fringe and pin and baste it to the inside edges of the mitred border, working neatly around the corners and leaving a 1 cm (½ in) seam allowance. The top of the fringe should lie about 3.5 cm (1½ in) from the outside edge of the mitred border.

10 To make up the front panel, cut four strips of tape into 36 cm (14½ in) lengths. Mitre the corners to form a square in the middle of the front panel, 3.5 cm (1½ in) from the raw edges. Hand sew a piece of braid down the middle of the tape. Machine stitch the tape to the front panel around both edges. Turn in and press a 1.5 cm (½ in) seam allowance.

11 Lay the front panel right side up so that it sits squarely inside the fringed inside edge of the mitred border. Pin, baste and use a small zigzag stitch to machine the front and back panels together.

12 To complete the back of the cushion, cut two slits for the buttonholes on the thicker side of the opening, cutting through both layers. Finish the slits with buttonhole stitch (see Techniques, page 102). Sew a button opposite each hole on the opposite side of the opening. Insert the cushion pad and fasten the buttons.

checked linen with contrast ties

Here, a generous beige linen flap tucks deep inside the outer checked casing, completely hiding the inner pad. Almost a slipcover in effect, and practical for slipping off for cleaning, it closes by means of two pairs of wide ties. The idea works equally effectively using the checked fabric as the inner flap and ties.

materials & equipment

50 cm (20 in) checked linen, 115 cm (45 in) wide

100 cm (40 in) plain linen, 115 cm (45 in) wide

140 cm (55 in) piping cord

45 cm (18 in) square cushion pad

1 For the front and back cover cut out two pieces of checked fabric measuring 48 x 48 cm (19 x 19 in). To make the inner flap, cut out one piece of plain linen measuring 48 x 20 cm (19 x 8 in) and for the inner facing cut out one piece of plain linen measuring 48 x 5 cm (19 x 2 in). For the ties, cut out four strips of plain linen each 34 x 14 cm (13½ x 5½ in). Cut out enough plain linen to make 140 cm (55 in) of piping (see Techniques, page 103).

2 To make the ties, fold each strip in half along the length with right sides together and machine stitch along the raw edges of the long side and one of the short ends, using a seam allowance of 1 cm (½ in). Turn the ties right side out through the open end and press.

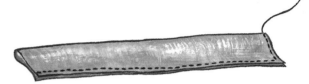

3 Lay the back panel right side up and line up the open ends of two of the ties with one of the raw edges at a distance of 9 cm (3½ in) from each corner. Pin and baste in place.

4 Lay the narrow strip of inner facing over the ties, right sides facing, matching the raw edges. Pin, baste and machine stitch along this edge through all layers, using a 1 cm (½ in) seam allowance. Turn the facing over to the wrong side of the checked fabric and press.

5 Turn under a 2 cm (¾ in) hem on the facing and machine stitch it down through all layers, making sure the stitching lines follow the line of the checks on the right side.

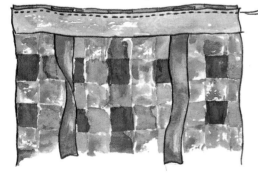

6 Take the front panel and lay it right side up. Place the remaining two ties along one of its raw edges, 9 cm (3½ in) from each corner. Pin and baste in place.

7 Lay the made-up piping along the other three sides of the right side of the front panel, lining up the raw edges. Pin, baste and machine stitch close to the piping cord.

8 Next take the inner flap. To make a neat hem, turn in 5 mm (¼ in) along one of the long edges and press. Turn in another 5 mm (¼ in) and press again. Machine stitch the hem in place.

9 Place the inner flap over the front panel right sides together. Line up the long raw edge with the unpiped top edge. Pin, baste and machine stitch this edge using a 1 cm (½ in) seam allowance. Turn the flap over and press it to the wrong side of the panel.

10 To assemble the cover, place the front and back panels right sides together. Pin, baste and machine stitch the three sides without ties together, using a 1 cm (½ in) seam allowance and making sure the piping cord remains on the inside of the stitching. The stitching at the bottom two corners should be rounded into a curve.

11 Trim the corners, then turn the cover right side out and press. Insert the cushion, tuck in the flap and fasten the ties in bows.

loose linen cover

Two squares of cool striped beige linen with pairs of ties on each side sandwich an inner cushion of contrasting striped fabric. A simple-to-make cushion which will make a big impact, this idea is excellent for giving a quick facelift to older cushions that are looking a little tired.

materials & equipment

60 cm (24 in) beige striped linen fabric, 115 cm (45 in) wide

50 cm (20 in) red striped cotton fabric, 115 cm (45 in) wide

500 cm (192 in) cotton tape in brown, 2.5 cm (1 in) wide

500 cm (192 in) cotton tape in cream, 1 cm (½ in) wide

45 cm (18 in) square cushion pad

1 For the outer cushion, cut out two pieces of fabric from the striped linen, each 55 cm (22 in) square. Make sure the stripes run parallel with two of the sides.

2 Take one of the pieces and fold in 5 mm (¼ in) all round, overlapping the corners. Then fold in 2 cm (¾ in) and press, making sure the stripes match up on the wrong side of the fabric. Repeat for the other piece.

3 To make the ties, place the narrow cream tape in the middle of the brown tape and machine stitch as close to the edges of the narrow tape as possible to secure together. Cut into 16 strips of 30 cm (12 in) lengths and press.

4 Lay one of the squares wrong side up and tuck one length of tape right side up 13 cm (5 in) from each corner, under the pressed edge. Pin ties into place.

5 To secure the ties to the cushion cover, machine stitch as close as possible to the inner edge of the turned-in seam, sewing across each of the ties. Make sure that the ties are straight.

6 Fold each tie over the seam and press. Machine a second line of stitching 5 mm (¼ in) in from the inner edge to secure the ties facing outwards. Press. Repeat to attach the ties to the other square. Slip stitch (see Techniques, page 101) each open corner closed and trim the ends of ties on the diagonal.

7 To make the inner cushion, cut out two pieces from the red striped cotton, each 48 cm (19 in) square. Lay the squares right sides together. Pin, baste and machine stitch a seam line 1 cm (½ in) in from the outside edge around three sides.

8 Turn the cover right side out and press. Insert the cushion pad and slip stitch the opening to a neat close.

9 Place the inner cushion in the middle of one outer panel (wrong side up), then put the other panel over it (wrong side down) and tie up to close.

surface decoration

For those who want to be challenged beyond running up cushions or covers on a sewing machine — or indeed for those who enjoy the slower pace of stitching by hand — there are numerous ways of applying surface decoration to your own or ready-made cushions. Cross stitch, embroidery, quilting and appliqué can all be used to add decorative and personal touches.

far left *Hand-stitched parallel rows of white knitting wool create a fine pattern on black wool.*

left *Black on white felt — painstakingly ordered circles have been cut out to provide the pattern on this white inner cushion.*

below left *Cream linen has been bordered in cross-stitched black embroidery thread; the back of the cushion is a black-and-white checked gingham.*

below *A brown boiled wool cushion has been embroidered with charming naive multicoloured flowers, and finished with thick red rope.*

bottom *A corner detail of a wool and velvet ribbon patchwork cushion.*

left *Embroidered leopard-skin tapestry looks like the real thing!*
below left to right *Strong yellow ovals of wool in satin stitch outlined in black. The most delicate flowers are intricately stiched onto cream linen. Leftover fabrics and a carefully cut initial appliquéd together.*
bottom left to right *Hand-painted silk makes an elegant cushion. The brown knitted cushion has been tie-dyed and felted to give a unique finish, while the top cushion is a patchwork of velvet ribbon, knitted wool squares and woven linen. A satin stitch embroidered heart in heavy wool on fine cream flannel.*

initials in cross stitch

What could be more personal than working someone's initials into a cushion design? Cross stitch is extremely simple, with lovely results. Here the cream edging on the scallops is echoed in the stitches. When you have decided on the initials you wish to stitch, map out an accurate chart to refer to and count rigorously; the chart is on page 104.

materials & equipment

50 cm (20 in) brown linen, 115 cm (45 in) wide

30 x 45 cm (12 x 18 in) cream felt

23 x 45 cm (9 x 18 in) rectangular cushion pad

cream stranded embroidery cotton

dressmaker's chalk

pinking shears

graph paper and pattern paper

embroidery needle

1 Cut two pieces of linen 48 x 25 cm (19 x 10 in) and use one of these pieces as a base for the cross stitch decoration. Trace the pattern onto graph paper and then transfer it onto the centre of the fabric (see the chart on page 104). Complete the design in cross stitch using the cream cotton thread.

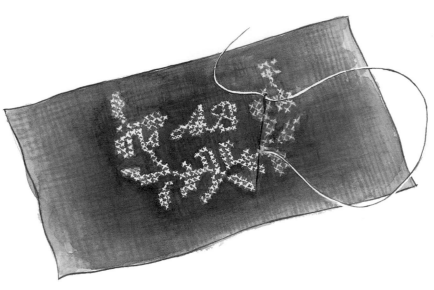

2 To make the scalloped edges, cut out one strip of brown linen measuring 15 x 48 cm (6 x 19 in) and two strips of cream felt measuring 15 x 45 cm (6 x 18 in). Make a template on a piece of pattern paper 8 x 47 cm (3 x 19 in). Draw four part-circles along the top of the paper with a 11.75 cm (4¾ in) diameter. Mark a point 4 cm (1½ in) from the bottom edge between each circle; draw a straight line through the points. For the scallops cut out the outline of the top half of each circle.

3 Take the linen strip and fold it in half lengthways, wrong sides facing. Lay the template over it, lining up the long straight edge with the long raw edges of the fabric and pin it down. Cut out the shapes, remove the paper and snip in between the scallops. Turn under 1 cm (½ in) along the curves and the two short ends of the strips and press.

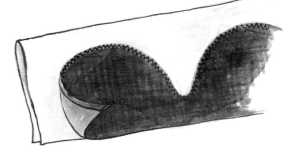

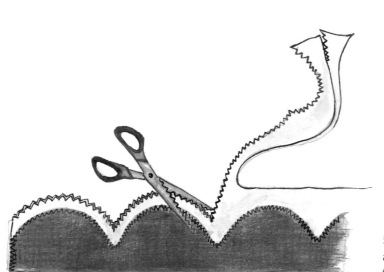

4 Fold the felt strips in half lengthways and place a linen piece on top of each one. Pin, baste and zigzag stitch the pieces together along the edge of the linen around the scallops and the short ends (see Techniques, page 102).

5 Using pinking shears, cut around the felt 1 cm (½ in) away from the linen.

6 To assemble the cushion, lay the embroidered front piece right side up and position the borders along each of the longer sides, with the felt facing up. Line up the raw edges and baste together using a seam allowance of 1 cm (½ in).

7 Place the back panel of linen on top of the front piece, right sides facing. Pin, baste and machine stitch along the two longer sides and one of the short ones using a 1 cm (½ in) seam allowance.

8 Turn the cover out, press it and insert the cushion pad. Slip stitch (see Techniques, page 101) the opening to a close.

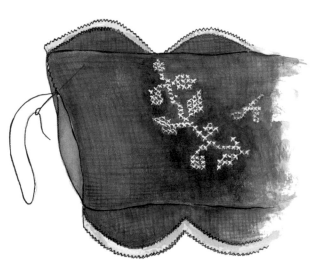

autumnal appliqué

Like many other forms of needlecraft, appliqué has survived for generations and lends itself particularly well to all manner of designs, pictorial or abstract. All you need to do is decide on a motif, or series of motifs, draw and cut them out from offcuts of fabric and apply them to a background. There is a template for the leaves on page 104.

materials & equipment

50 cm (20 in) heavy cotton fabric, 115 cm (45 in) wide

25 cm (10 in) contrasting fabric for the motif, 115 cm (45 in) wide

45 cm (18 in) square cushion pad

25 cm (10 in) iron-on adhesive webbing, 115 cm (45 in) wide

tracing paper

1 Cut out two pieces of the heavy cotton fabric, each measuring 48 x 48 cm (19 x 19 in), for the front and back panels. Make sure the grain of the fabric is straight, not diagonal.

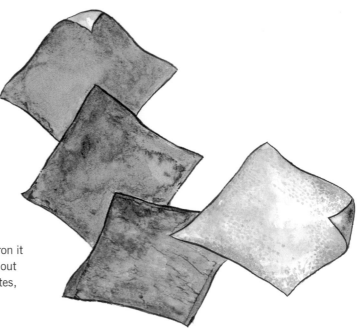

2 Take the piece of contrasting fabric and iron it smoothly onto the adhesive webbing and cut out four squares to fit the leaf motifs (see Templates, page 104).

3 Draw the shapes of the appliqué leaf motifs on the tracing paper, increasing the proportions to the desired size. Cut them out, and lay them over the contrasting fabric squares. Secure them in place with pins and carefully cut out each leaf.

4 Remove the paper and adhere the leaves to the right side of one of the cotton pieces. Machine stitch them in place, close to the edges, using a top stitch.

5 To decorate the leaves, machine stitch the outline of the veins and the stalks in a different coloured thread using a tight zigzag stitch.

6 To assemble the cover lay the remaining piece of cotton over the appliquéd piece, with right sides together. Pin, baste and machine stitch along three sides, using a seam allowance of 1 cm (½ in).

7 Turn to the right side, insert the cushion pad and slip stitch (see Techniques, page 101) the open end closed.

equipment and techniques

sewing kit

For the projects in this book you will need some basic tools. A few good scissors, including a pair of large, cutting-out shears, medium-size dressmaker's scissors and small embroidery scissors for snipping threads. Pinking shears are useful for finishing raw edges and making decorative edgings. Use good-quality steel dressmaking pins that will not rust or go blunt; keep them in a box so they stay sharp. Choose your needle according to the weight of the fabric and the thickness of the thread, and use a special needle for embroidery. An iron is invaluable during the making-up process but should be used with a damp cloth to protect delicate fabrics. Other useful items to have to hand are a seam ripper to unpick seams, a blunt knitting needle or pair of tweezers for pushing out corners, and a thimble.

measuring and marking tools

Use a long, straight ruler together with a tape measure, and double-check all measurements. When it comes to drawing up circular or star shapes and smooth curves use a compass and protractor or a length of string attached to a pencil at one end with a pin at the other to act as a pivot. For specific designs that need to be scaled up and down, use graph paper; you can purchase special paper for cutting out templates. When marking up a fabric, dressmaker's chalk is easy to apply and remove, and comes in a variety of colours to suit your fabric. Alternatively use contrasting basting cotton to make several small, loose loops, or tailor's tacks which can be snipped away without trace. If you use a marker pen test it first to ensure it leaves absolutely no mark on the right side of the fabric.

fabrics

In each project the fabrics are specified, as the weight, texture and pattern is suited to the particular design. Stick to a similar weight of fabric if you choose an alternative. Choose the type of fabric according to the function of the cushion. Use general furnishing fabrics for most cushions, tougher cloth for floor, outdoor or squab cushions and delicate fabrics for more decorative cushions. Check how much a fabric is likely to shrink, as you may need to buy up to a third more material to compensate for this; if possible pick a colourfast cloth. Machine wash the fabric to pre-shrink it before starting the project, in case different sections shrink at different rates. For borders and back panels of cushions you can join sections of fabric that are not quite large enough by carefully matching up the pattern.

pads and fillings

Ready-made cushion pads come in a variety of shapes and sizes and with different fillings. The most luxurious filling is feather and down, which should be used sparingly in a puffy scatter cushion or more densely to stuff a firm seat cover. If you make your own cushion pad with a feather filling use a downproof fabric such as a thick, close-weave cotton, otherwise sharp feather ends will protrude. Plain cotton or calico fabric is suitable for pads with a synthetic filling. Do not allow feather or synthetic pads to get wet as they are very absorbent. Plastic or latex foam chips are lumpy and uncomfortable but non-absorbent, so are useful for outdoor furnishings. Foam blocks can be cut to size and are used to form squabs for seating; cover the blocks with wadding first to smooth out the corners.

techniques

The sewing techniques in the projects featured involve both hand and machine stitches; the more complicated ones are outlined below. All the cushions can be completed however by using a backstitch. When marking and measuring fabric make sure you work in either imperial or metric.

running or gathering stitch

A series of small, neat stitches, equal in length on both sides of the fabric. Running stitch is used to gather cloth by hand. Knot the thread at one end and sew two parallel rows of running stitches close together along the length to be gathered. Wind the loose threads at the other end around a pin and pull gently to form even gathers.

slip stitch

A simple way to join two folded edges. Knot the end of the thread and working from right to left insert the needle and slip it through the fold for about 5 mm (¼ in). On the other piece of fabric pick up a couple of threads to join the two edges. The stitches should be almost invisible, so keep them small. Slip stitch is easy to unpick if, say, you want to remove a cushion cover for washing.

back stitch

This creates a firm join that can be used as an alternative to machine stitching, or for finishing thread ends securely by sewing a few stitches on top of one another, as an alternative to making a knot. After completing a stitch insert the needle at the end of the previous stitch, bring it out a stitch length in front of the thread to create a solid line of stitching on the right side and an overlapping effect on the underside.

cross stitch

Where possible, work decorative cross stitches in a line, first stitching half the cross before returning back along the line to complete the stitch. Make sure that the top stitches of the cross all slant in the same direction.

feather stitch

Work this decorative stitch on the right side of the fabric. Bring the needle through at a, insert at b, bring through again at c, looping the thread under the needle before pulling it through. Mirror the process by inserting the needle at d, coming out at e and looping the thread under the needle once again. Repeat this pattern, alternating the looped stitches on either side of the central line.

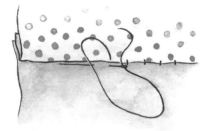

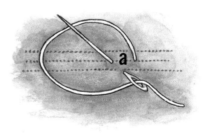

hem stitch

Use this stitch to hold a folded edge to flat fabric. Sewing a hem by hand produces a much neater result than machine hemming. On the wrong side catch a couple of threads from the flat fabric; with the needle pointing diagonally from right to left slide it under the folded edge and bring it up through both layers of the fold. Most hems are turned under twice, but for heavy fabrics make a single turn, after finishing the exposed raw edge (see page 102).

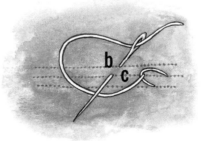

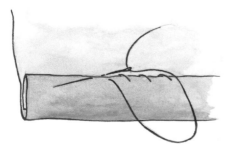

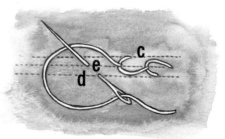

blanket stitch

A decorative stitch for neatening edges. Secure the thread at one end of the fabric and working from right to left insert the needle about 1 cm (½ in) from the edge; keep the thread under the point of the needle and complete the stitch to create a loop. Continue to work the stitches every 1 cm (½ in) or so, making sure the height is even.

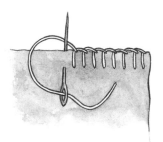

buttonhole stitch

This stitch is both decorative and strengthening as it prevents fraying of the cut to accommodate the button. Some machines have a buttonhole stitch attachment. Work on the right side using a short needle and a strong thread with a knotted end. Hide the knot on the wrong side of the fabric and work with the cut edge on the right (on the left if you are left-handed). Insert the needle at right angles to the cut edge, taking a stitch through the fabric, loop the thread behind the needle before pulling through to form a knot on the cut edge with each stitch. Keep the stitches evenly spaced, maintain an even tension on each knot and aim for the knots to touch each other. Fan the stitches close together around both ends of the hole, to prevent tearing. The more the fabric frays the deeper your stitches should be.

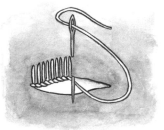

seams

Stitch seams from top to bottom, making sure that patterned fabrics run the same way on either side of the join. The most commonly used seam is the flat seam; place the fabric right sides together with raw edges matching and pin, baste and machine stitch to join, making a few back stitches to secure the threads at the end. For heavy fabrics trim the seam allowance close to the stitching to reduce bulk. If the seam is to be pressed to one side use a grading technique by cutting only one seam allowance back to create a smoother surface on the right side of the material. If the cloth is likely to fray finish the raw edges (see below).

finishing seams

There are three ways to finish seams to neaten and strengthen them. On fabric which is not liable to fray, you can either leave the seam allowance untrimmed, although you should neaten the corners (see below), or else pink the raw edges with pinking shears. To finish a seam by hand use oversewing or overcasting. To finish a raw edge by machine you can use a small and narrow zigzag, working the zigzag part over the raw edge or overlocking, which consists of a zigzag followed by two straight stitches.

neatening corners and curves

Although it is not strictly necessary to finish seams as the allowances lie inside the cushion cover and are not visible, for good results you should pay some attention to corners and curves. To create a neat pointed corner, stitch right up to the corner, leave the needle in the fabric, raise the machine foot and pivot the fabric through 90º, then lower the foot and continue stitching. Trim the seam allowance across the corner so you can push the finished corner out to a neat point. For sharp angles (such as the star project on page 12) machine one or two stitches across the point to strengthen it.

When sewing a curved seam keep a uniform seam allowance. For concave (inward-facing) curves snip little notches to achieve a flat finish. For convex (outward-facing) curves cut small slits into the seam allowance.

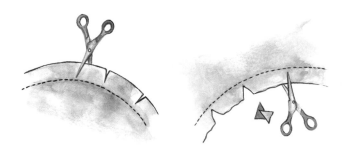

bias binding and piping

'Bias binding' is the term given to strips of fabric cut on the diagonal grain that is used to cover piping cord. Both bias binding and piping cord are available ready-made but you can create much more versatile matching or contrasting trimmings by making up your own. Choose a fabric of the same type and weight as the body of the cushion to avoid problems of shrinking and bunching after washing. 'Flat piping' refers to a bias strip used folded in half without the cord inserted. Piping cord is available in different thickness so choose an appropriate width. For safety, wash cotton cord before you begin sewing to pre-shrink it, or the piping may pucker later. Likewise, make sure that purchased piping and bias binding are shrinkproof and colourfast before sewing. To make bias strips, take a square of fabric and fold a straight raw edge parallel to the selvedge (the non-fray woven edge) to form a triangle. The bottom of the triangle is the bias line. Use a long ruler and dressmaker's chalk to mark out a series of lines parallel to the bias line, according to the width you require. Calculate the length of piping required and join enough strips to cover the cord. The bias must be wide enough to cover the cord comfortably with an additional 1 cm (½ in) seam allowance.

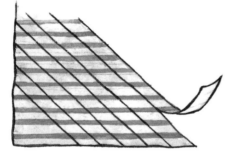

Cut out and join bias strips right sides together along the short ends with a flat seam. Press the seam and trim the corners to lie flat with the bias strip.

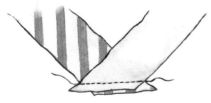

Place the bias strip wrong side up and fold evenly in half around the piping cord. Pin and baste to close, then machine or use back stitch (see page 101) to secure.

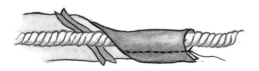

Apply the piping along the seam line between two pieces Apply the piping along the seam line between two pieces of fabric. Snip the seam allowance on the bias strip up to the stitching to help turn corners. Where the piped edges meet trim down the cord so the ends butt together and trim the fabric strip so there is an overlap of 1 cm (½ in); turn under one end for 5 mm (¼ in) and tuck the opposite raw edge inside; stitch across the join.

transferring a design

If your pattern is actual size it can be traced directly onto the tracing and transfer paper. If it has to be enlarged transfer the pattern onto graph paper and increase the proportion to the desired size; alternatively use a photocopier to enlarge. After you have done this rule horizontal and vertical lines through the centre of the design. To transfer a design onto the front of a cushion cover, iron the piece of cloth you are going to embroider on and fold it in half vertically. Open out the fold and sew a straight line of basting stitches down the middle. Repeat to divide and mark the cloth in half along the horizontal to give you a guide for plotting the pattern.

Use transfer paper or special dressmaker's carbon which is a non-smudge carbon paper that comes in several colours and is available from most haberdashers. Choose a paper that contrasts well with the fabric you are going to embroider on so that the design shows up clearly. Place the fabric right side up on a hard surface and place the transfer paper shiny side down over it. Place the tracing paper over the transfer paper and line up the horizontal and vertical lines already marked before pinning all three layers together. Trace over the design with a ballpoint pen or a pencil. Carefully remove the tracing and transfer papers and begin to cross stitch (see page 101) following the imprint of the design left on the fabric. Always work from the centre outwards. The cross stitches should extend slightly beyond the carbon paper lines so they are not visible on the finished fabric. Remove the basting stitches once the embroidery is complete.

For the design on the next page, (featured in the initials in cross stitch project, page 92) it is necessary to double the size of the pattern before transferring it to the fabric; use one of the methods explained earlier in Transferring a design, above. To add a personal touch to your embroidered cushion insert the initials of your choice instead of using the ones given. To do this, leave a gap where the A and the B are and replace them with small crosses marking your new letters.

Use these two templates for the autumnal appliqué project featured on page 96; they must be doubled in size (see Transferring a design, page 103) before being used to cut out the fabric.

directory of suppliers

Fabric and trimmings suppliers

Alton-Brooke
Chelsea Harbour Design Centre
London SW10 OXE
Tel: 020 7376 7008

B.Brown-Muraspec
Zoffany House, 74–78 Wood Lane End
Hemel Hempstead
Herts. HP2 4RF
Tel: 08705 117 118
www.mursapec.co.uk

The Blue Door
74 Church Road
London SW13 ODQ
Tel: 020 8748 9785
www.bluedoorbarnes.co.uk

Cath Kidston
8 Clarendon Cross
London W11 4AP
Tel: 020 7221 4000
www.cathkidston.co.uk

Chelsea Textiles
7 Walton Street
London SW3 2JD
Tel: 020 7584 0111
www.chelseatextiles.com

Colefax & Fowler
110 Fulham Road
London SW3 6XL
Tel: 020 7244 7427

The Conran Shop
81 Fulham Road
London SW3 6RD
Tel: 020 7589 7401
www.conran.com

Crowson Monkwell
227 King's Road
London SW3 5EJ
Tel: 020 7823 3294
www.crowsonfabrics.com

Designers Guild
277 Kings Road
London SW3 5EN
Tel: 020 7243 7300
www.designersguild.com

GP & J Baker
Unit 18–19
   Chelsea Harbour Design Centre
London SW10 OXE
Tel: 020 7351 7760
www.gpjbaker.co.uk

Hodsoll McKenzie
52 Pimlico Road
London SW1W 8LP
Tel: 020 7730 2877
www.hodsollmckenzie.com

Ian Mankin
109 Regent's Park Road
London NW1 8UR
Tel: 020 7722 0997

JAB International
Chelsea Harbour Design Centre
London SW10 OXE
Tel: 020 7349 9323
www.jab.de

Jane Churchill
151 Sloane Street
London SW1 X 9BX
Tel: 020 7730 9847

Lee Jofa
Unit 18/19 Chelsea Harbour Design Centre
London SW10 OXE
Tel: 020 7351 7760
www.leejofa.com

Manuel Canovas
110 Fulham Road
London SW3 6RL
Tel: 020 7244 7427

Osborne & Little
304 King's Road
London SW3 5UH
Tel: 020 7352 1456
www.osborneandlittle.com

Pierre Frey
251–253 Fulham Road
London SW3 6HY
Tel: 020 7376 5599
www.pierrefrey.com

Sahco Hesslein
G24 Chelsea Harbour Design Centre
London SW10 OXE
Tel: 020 7352 6168
www.sahco-hesslein.com

Sanderson
233 King's Road
London SW3 5EJ
Tel: 020 7351 7728
www.sanderson-online.co.uk

Shaker
Tel: 020 7935 9461
www.shaker.co.uk

Turnell & Gigon
G20 Chelsea Harbour Design Centre
London SW10 OXE
Tel: 020 8971 1711

Wendy Cushing Trimmings
Chelsea Harbour Design Centre
London SW10 OXE
Tel: 020 7351 5796

V. V. Rouleaux
54 Sloane Square
Cliveden Place
London SW1W 8AX
Tel: 020 7730 3125
www.vvrouleaux.com

Zoffany
G9 Chelsea Harbour Design Centre
London SW10 OXE
Tel: 020 7349 0043
www.zoffany.uk.com

Cushion suppliers

The Blue Door
74 Church Road
London SW13 ODQ
Tel: 020 8748 9785
www.bluedoorbarnes.co.uk

Cath Kidston
8 Clarendon Cross
London W11 4AP
Tel: 020 7221 4000
www.cathkidston.co.uk

Chelsea Textiles
7 Walton Street
London SW3 2JD
Tel: 020 7584 0111
www.chelseatextiles.com

Guinevere Antiques
674 King's Road
London SW6 2DY
Tel: 020 7736 2917
www.guinevere.co.uk

Habitat
Tel: 0870 411 5500
www.habitat.co.uk

Harrods
Knightsbridge
London SW1X 7XL
Tel: 020 7730 1234
www.harrods.com

Hikaru Noguchi Textile Design
Unit E4 Cockpit Workshops
Cockpit Yard
London WC1N 2NP
Tel: 020 7813 1227
www.hikarunoguchi.com

Ikea
www.ikea.com

John Lewis
Tel: 08456 049 049
www.johnlewis.com

Liberty
210 Regent Street
London W1R 6AH
Tel: 020 7734 1234
www.liberty.co.uk

Mulberry Home
322 King's Road
London SW3 5UH
Tel: 020 7823 3455
www.leejofa.com

Shaker
Tel: 020 7935 9461
www.shaker.co.uk

Tobias & the Angel
68 White Hart Lane
Barnes
London SW13 OPZ
Tel: 020 8878 8902

credits

page 1   bottom left and right: cushion from Liberty; fabric from Colefax & Fowler; top cushion made by Hikaru Noguchi

page 2   from top to bottom: cushion from Liberty; cushion made by Hikaru Noguchi; fabric from Manuel Canovas; silk from JAB; tweed from Liberty

page 4   from top to bottom: fabric from Turnell & Gigon; fabric from Chelsea Textiles; cushion made by Celia Dewes; fabric from Colefax & Fowler, trimmings by V. V. Rouleaux; centre: fabric by Schumacher from Turnell & Gigon, tassel from Wendy Cushing

page 5   right: fabric from Chelsea Textiles, trimmings by V. V. Rouleaux

page 7   all cushions from Cath Kidston

pages 8–9   clockwise from top: heart fabric from GP & J Baker, trimming from Osborne and Little; large check fabric from Colefax & Fowler; triangular fabrics from GP & J Baker; stripe fabric from Sanderson, trimming from V. V. Rouleaux; star check fabric from Chelsea Textiles; stripe and plain fabric from Sanderson; plaid from Colefax & Fowler.

page 100   cushion from The Blue Door

page 105   from top to bottom: fabric from The Conran Shop; silk from JAB; cushion from Liberty; fabric from Zoffany, trimming by Nina Campbell at Osborne & Little; fabric from Osborne & Little, trimming from V. V. Rouleaux

page 106   from left to right: fabric by Schumacher from Turnell & Gigon, tassels from V. V. Rouleaux; fabric from Zoffany, tassels from Wendy Cushing

page 110   fabric from John Lewis; fringe and tufted buttons from Colefax & Fowler

page 111   antique cushion from Antiques & Things

page 112   fabric from Lee Jofa

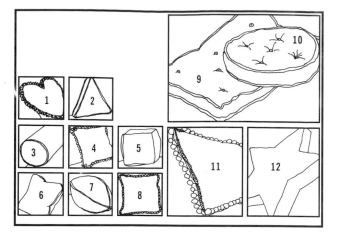

shapes pages 10–11
1   fabric from GP & J Baker, trimming from Osborne & Little
2   fabric from GP & J Baker
3, 6, 8, 9   fabrics from Colefax & Fowler
5, 7, 10   fabrics from Osborne & Little
4   fabric from GP & J Baker, trimming from Jane Churchill
11   fabric from Sanderson, trimming from V. V. Rouleaux
12   fabric from Chelsea Textiles

projects: the star: fabric from Chelsea Textiles • bee bolster: fabric from Chelsea Textiles • striped tufted mattress: fabric from Turnell & Gigon • bobbles in the round: fabric from The Conran Shop, bobble fringe from Jane Churchill

use of fabrics pages 28–29
1   fabric from Colefax & Fowler, trimming from Osborne & Little
2   cushion made by Hikaru Noguchi
3   cushion from Mulberry Home
4, 5, 7, 8, 9, 11, 12   cushions from Harrods
6   fabric from Zoffany, trimming from Osborne & Little
8   fabric from Liberty
10   cushion from Guinevere Antiques

projects: stripes into squares: fabric from Turnell & Gigon, tassel from Wendy Cushing • basket weave of ribbons: made by Hikaru Noguchi • floppy stone-washed silk: fabric from Alton-Brooke • patchwork puzzle: from Tobias & The Angel

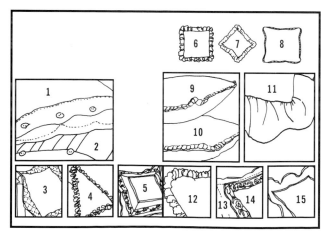

borders and edgings pages 46–47
1, 2, 5, 8, 14   cushions from The Blue Door
3   printed and plain fabric from Colefax & Fowler, embroidery linen from John Lewis
4   fabric from John Lewis, trimming from V. V. Rouleaux
6   fabrics from John Lewis
7   fabric and bias binding from John Lewis
9, 10   fleece and thread from John Lewis
11   both fabrics from Sanderson
12   fabric from Crowson Monkwell
13   cushion from Tobias & the Angel
15   fabric from The Blue Door

projects: scallops and zigzags: fabrics from John Lewis • box-pleated border: fabric from Sahco Hesslein • double ruffle taffeta: fabric from Pierre Frey • double-flanged border: fabrics from GP & J Baker

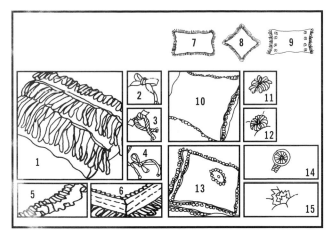

trimmings and fastenings pages 64–65
1   trimming from V. V. Rouleaux
2   fabric from Crowson Monkwell
3   fabric from Turnell & Gigon
4   fabric from The Blue Door
5   fabric from JAB, trimming from V. V. Rouleaux
6   fabric from The Conran Shop, trimming from
    Wendy Cushing
7   fabric from Sahco Hesslein, trimming from V. V. Rouleaux
8   fabric and trimmings from John Lewis
9   fabric from John Lewis, trimmings from Colefax & Fowler
10 cushion from Chelsea Textiles
11 12 tufts from Colefax & Fowler
13 fabric from Osborne & Little, trimming from V. V. Rouleaux
14 antique button
15 fabric from Colefax & Fowler

projects: rope-edged knotted cushion: inspired by Wendy Harrop,
fabric from Ian Mankin, rope border from John Lewis • fastened with
tassels: inner fabric from Manuel Canovas, outer fabric from John
Lewis, tassels from Wendy Cushing • the envelope cushion: fabric
from Sanderson, trimmings from John Lewis • all trimmed: fabric from
Colefax & Fowler, trimmings from V. V. Rouleaux • checked linen with
contrast ties: check fabric from Turnell & Gigon, plain from John Lewis
• loose linen cover: fabrics from Sanderson, ties from John Lewis

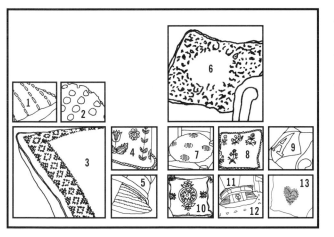

surface decoration pages 90–91
1, 7   fabric and trimmings from John Lewis
2   cushion from Margret Adolfsdottir
3   cushion embroidered by Gillian Bowden
4   cushion from Tobias and the Angel
5, 11   cushion made by Hikaru Noguchi from Timney & Fowler
6, 10   cushions from Harrods
8   cushion from Chelsea Textiles
9   spotted fabric from Designer's Guild, striped fabric from
    Hodsoll McKenzie
12 cushion made by Jo Sheffield
13 cushion made by Celia Dewes

projects: initials in cross stitch: fabric from Manuel Canovas, felt from
B. Brown • autumnal appliqué: fabrics from John Lewis

glossary

Adhesive webbing
Paper-backed sticky material attached to fabric for added strength.

Basting
Large straight stitches used to fasten fabric temporarily.

Braid
A woven ribbon used to trim or edge pillows and cushions.

Carpet webbing
Strong closely woven tape used to support upholstery or cut into lengths to form ties.

Chenille
Tufty and soft velvety yarn; wool cotton or synthetic.

Cotton
A natural fibre made from the boll of the cotton plant, producing strong and durable yarn.

Crewel work
Large-scale embroidery.

Damask
A reversible figured woven fabric, usually silk, satin or linen.

Drawn thread work
Ornamental work done by removing threads in one direction and grouping the rest with a thicker thread.

Facing
A section of material added for strength or contrast.

Felt
Unwoven cloth made from pounded wool; the edges do not fray after cutting.

Figured material
Fabric with a pattern, formed by the weave structure.

Filo floss cotton
A six-stranded plied silk thread.

Flange
A projecting flat rim or border.

Gathers
Puckers or folds made by drawing on a loosely stitched thread.

Gaufrage
A pattern branded onto the surface of velvet.

Interlining
Soft material, used as backing or inner lining.

Kapok
Fluffy, fine stuffing material.

Knife pleat
A narrow flat pleat.

Linen
Fibres spun from flax to produce a strong, thick and flexible fabric.

Madras cotton
Striped and checked fine Indian cotton, usually in bright colours.

Mitre
The diagonal join of two pieces of fabric formed at a corner.

Muslin
A sheer, strong but delicately woven fabric.

Organdie
A fine, sheer and crisp fabric made with cotton yarns.

Organza
A thin, plain-woven silk or synthetic fabric with a stiff finish.

Provençal print
French country prints on cotton, characterized by brightly coloured and small motifs.

Raw edge
The cut edge of fabric, without selvedge or hem; often needs finishing to prevent fraying.

Satin
Silk, cotton or synthetic fabric with a smooth, glossy surface and a dull back.

Satin stitch
An embroidery stitch used to fill a design.

Seam allowance
The narrow strip of raw-edged fabric left when making a seam, to allow for fraying.

Seam line
The line formed when two pieces of material are stitched together.

Selvedge
The defined warp edge of the fabric, specially woven to prevent unravelling.

Silk
Luxurious, strong fabric produced by silkworms.

Squab
A thick box-shaped cushion pad.

Stone-washed silk
Faded silk produced by washing with abrasives.

Stranded cotton
A six-stranded thread with a sheen; used for embroidery.

Template
A card or paper shape, used to mark specific outlines on fabric.

Tie-dyed cloth
A texture and pattern produced after resist printing.

Toile
Plain cloth on its own or in Toile de Jouy to mean fabric embellished with pictorial scenes.

Top stitch
A straight seam, showing on the right side of the fabric.

Velvet
A rich fabric, usually made of cotton or synthetic fibre, with a thick and soft warp-pile.

Wadding
Soft, pliable, cotton lining material.

Weave
An interlacing action used to form something such as a fabric.

Width
The distance from selvedge to selvedge on any fabric. The standard widths are 90 cm (36 in), 115 cm (45 in) and 150 cm (60 in).

index

adhesive webbing 96, 98
appliqué 90, 91, 96–99

back stitch 101, 102, 103
basting 15, 18, 19, 103, 104
bias binding 46, 47, 103,
blanket stitch 102
bolsters 10, 16, 19, 28
borders and edgings 46–63
  bobble 28
  box pleated 52, 55
  double gathered 47
  double ruffle 56, 59, 64
  double flanged 60–63
braid 16, 19, 28, 78, 81
buttonhole stitch 73, 81, 102
buttons 10, 47, 65, 74, 77, 78,
  81

calico 100
carpet webbing 86
chenille fringes 10, 28
corners, neatening 102
cotton 10, 15, 28, 30–33,
  52–55, 64, 66–69, 96–99,
  100
crewel work 65
cross stitch 90, 92, 94, 101,
  104
curves, neatening, 102

damask 28, 29, 46
drawn thread work 70, 72

embroidery 6, 90, 91, 103, 104
equipment 100–102

fabrics, use of 28–45, 100
  crazy velvet patchwork 42–45
  floppy-edged cushion 38–41
  ribbon weave 34–37
  see also individual fabrics
feather stitch 42, 45, 101
felt 29, 90, 91, 92, 94
figured silk 60–63
fillings 100
flanges 60–63
flannel 91
flaps 47, 51, 60, 63, 74, 76, 77,
  82, 84
frills 46
fringes 10, 11, 24–27, 28, 64,
  65, 78, 81

gathering stitch 59, 101
gathers 41, 58
gaufrage 28

hem stitch 101
hessian 29, 46,

initials 6, 92–94, 104
interlining 34–37

kapok stuffing 12, 15
knitted cushions 91
knotted cushion 66–69

linen 10, 11, 20, 23, 46, 47,
  48, 64, 65, 70–73, 74–77,
  78–81, 82–85, 86–89,
  90–95

Madras cotton 66–69
marking tools 100

mattress effect 6, 10, 20–23
measuring tools 100
mitre 30, 32, 40, 46, 80, 81
mohair 28
muslin 24–27
needlepoint 29

organdie 28
organza 46
overcasting stitch 45, 102
oversewing 102

pads 100
patchwork 42–45, 65, 90, 91
piping 103
pleats 16–19, 52–55, 64

quilting 90
quilting 20, 23

ribbon 28, 29, 46, 64, 90, 91
ribbon weave 34–37
ruffles 56–59, 64
running stitch 27, 41, 68, 101

satin 64
satin stitch 91
scallops 48–50, 92–95
seams 102
sewing kit 100
shapes 10–26
  bolster 10, 16–19, 28
  box cube 11
  heart-shaped 10
  rectangular 10, 11
  rugby ball 11
  square 10, 11
  star 11, 12–15

mattress 20–23
  triangular 10, 46
silk 28, 38, 41, 42, 60–63, 64,
  70–73, 91
slip stitch 15, 19, 22, 23, 26,
  45, 55, 62, 63, 69, 73, 77,
  89, 95, 99, 101
squab 20–23, 100
stab stitch 23

taffeta 56–59
tapestry 91
tassels 28, 29, 30, 33, 34, 70,
  73, 74, 77
techniques 103–104
template 14, 44, 50, 68, 94, 96,
  98, 104
tie-died cloth 91
ties 30, 33, 51, 64, 82–85,
  86–89
top stitch 41, 99
transferring a design 103–104
tufts 20, 23, 64
Turkish corners 11

uses of cushions
  on hard seats 6, 10, 20
  as support 6, 16
  use of colour 6, 11, 30

velvet 28, 29, 34–36, 42–45
velvet ribbon 90, 91
viscose 11

wool 28, 78, 90, 91

zigzag stitch 40, 80, 94, 99
zigzags 48, 64

acknowledgements

Without the goodwill, trust and kindness of the press offices of all the fabric suppliers mentioned in the credits we would not have had very much to photograph for this book; to you all, many thanks. All at Ryland Peters & Small who have worked hard on this project, especially Jacqui, Anne, David, Ingunn, Sophie and Sian — what a team! James Merrell's unflagging enthusiasm and gorgeous pictures are always appreciated. Heartfelt thanks go to Catherine Coombes, who has not only been an invaluable assistant, but has also held together the home front during shoots — always with a positive, sweet, and cheery disposition. Thanks go also to the kind people who let us use their homes to photograph in, and to all the people who helped by lending goods or being otherwise helpful during this project: Isobel Bird, Trudi Ballard, Gillian Bowden, Celia Dewes, Cath Kidston, Angel Hughes, Catharina Mannerfelt, Hikaru Noguchi, Annie Stevens and Susie Tinsley. And finally thanks to my boys; David, my husband, Harry, our son; and Daisy, the family mut.

dedication

For Hänsi Schneider, with love and gratitude